Belfast International Airport

Belfast International Airport

Aviation at Aldergrove since 1918

Guy Warner & Jack Woods

6 5 4 3 2 1

© Guy Warner and Jack Woods
Newtownards 2001
Text: Guy Warner
Photographic Editor: Jack Woods

Designed by Colourpoint Books,
Newtownards
Printed by W & G Baird Ltd

ISBN 1 898392 66 8 (paperback)
       1 898392 68 4 (hardback)

Colourpoint Books
Unit D5, Ards Business Centre
Jubilee Road
NEWTOWNARDS
County Down
Northern Ireland
BT23 4YH
Tel: 028 9182 0505
Fax: 028 9182 1900
E-mail: Info@colourpoint.co.uk
Web-site: www.colourpoint.co.uk

Guy Warner has been a regular contributor to *Ulster Airmail*, the journal of the Ulster Aviation Society, for five years and has also written for *Air Britain Digest*, *Aircraft Illustrated*, *Air Enthusiast*, *Air Pictorial*, *Aviation Ireland* and *Northern Ireland Travel News*. He is a member of the Ulster Aviation Society, the Aviation Society of Ireland and Air Britain – the International Society of Aviation Historians. Guy is a teacher at Ben Madigan Prep School in Belfast. He is married with two daughters and lives in Greenisland, Co Antrim.

Guy is the co-author of *In the Heart of the City: The History of Belfast's City Airport, 1938–1998* and *Flying from Malone: Belfast's First Civil Aerodrome.*

Jack Woods has been an industrial photographer for 25 years, 20 of which have been with Short Brothers of Belfast. He is a member of the Master Photography Association. From his schooldays he has maintained an interest in aviation, and has been involved with the Ulster Aviation Society for the past 24 years. He is also a member of the Irish Aviation Society and Air Britain. Jack has contributed photographs and articles to aviation magazines in the UK, the Republic of Ireland, America, Australia and New Zealand. Jack also has a keen interest in the industrial history of Ulster and is a committee member of Friends of Cultra, an organisation affiliated to the Ulster Folk and Transport Museum.

Jack is the co-author of *In the Heart of the City: The History of Belfast's City Airport, 1938–1998* and *Flying from Malone: Belfast's First Civil Aerodrome.*

Cover and Frontispiece Illustrations

Front Cover:
Background – Belfast International from the air (*J Woods*).
Top Left – Avro Anson of 502 Squadron (*RG Spencer*).
Middle – Sabena BAe 146 (*J Woods*).
Bottom – Vickers VC-10 of BOAC (*S Boyd*).

Back Cover:
Top – BIA check-in hall (*J Woods*).
Bottom – Belfast International corridor carpet (*Belfast International Airport*).

Frontispiece:
The entrance to Aldergrove in the 1920s (*E Cromie Collection*).

Contents

Foreword vi

Preface vii

Acknowledgements viii

Map of Northern Ireland ix

Maps of Aldergrove/BIA x

1 The First Decade 1

2 From 502 to WW2 11

3 Aldergrove at War 28

4 Post-War Days 38

5 A New Civil Airport for Northern Ireland 49

6 The 1960s 57

7 The 1970s 73

8 The 1980s 84

9 The 1990s 98

10 TBI and the Future 118

Appendix 1: Operational Facilities 128

Appendix 2: Airlines, Routes and Aircraft 129

Appendix 3: Aircraft used by Local Air Companies 132

Appendix 4: Passenger and Freight Figures 133

Notes 134

Sources and Bibliography 135

Index 137

Foreword

Three years in the last 80 doesn't sound like such a long time, especially when one thinks of all that occurred during the twentieth century. However, those three years for me represent both a lifetime and yet a brief moment in time. I had the privilege to serve as the last managing director of the twentieth century. There is much that has happened at Belfast International and RAF Aldergrove. The airfield was one of the first on the island, and has seen dramatic changes in technology, both on the ground and in the air, as well as the economic, political and social changes that have occurred.

This is the story of an airfield that became an airport and is now a major economic generator for the province of Northern Ireland. In April 2000, the airport had an annual throughput of 3.1 million passengers, 100,000 aircraft movements, 41,000 tonnes of airfreight and employed some 3,000 people. The biggest carriers are British Midland, British Airways, easyJet, Airtours and Air 2000, with DHL, TNT, Air Contractors and Emerald providing the bulk of the freight activity. It mustn't be forgotten that there are military personnel and their families at RAF Aldergrove who form part of the NATO defence shield and share facilities with the airport. The growth of the civil activity at the airport is set to continue, despite continuing competition from Belfast City and Dublin.

BIA is many people's first and last glimpse of Northern Ireland and TBI plc has invested in the airport to ensure that it remains at the forefront of regional airport operations around the world. At the time of writing this foreword, a major redevelopment of the International Pier has just been completed and work was about to commence on additions to the cargo complex and aprons. More investment means more jobs, and greater prosperity will, I am sure, lead to

political stability and peace. Peace will lead to more passengers and more activity will lead to further prosperity. Hopefully, a virtual spiral of success will have been created which will benefit the community as whole.

However, history is about time. Time is a human concept and therefore, whilst this book is written about an airport, it really is about the people and the events that have shaped its destiny. Guy Warner and Jack Woods first approached me in 1998 about the possibility of undertaking a book about the airport. I didn't believe that they would be able to find sufficient information. However, they proved me wrong. I commend this book to you as it contains much history, anecdotes and some Belfast International/Aldergrove mythology. Jack Woods' photographs do justice to the current facilities and modern day aircraft.

In peace and war Belfast International/Aldergrove has played its part and I am proud that I was able to play a very small role in its history. I can look back over the three years I spent at BIA with great fondness. I had a most enjoyable time working with some of the best professionals in the business. Not only did we manage to add 600,000 extra passengers to the airport throughput, we doubled the profit and, despite the long hours and hard work, had some fun too.

I have seen this book through from its genesis to completion and have begun to realise just how much effort and determination was required on behalf of the authors to produce it. I hope you will enjoy reading it.

Paul Kehoe
London
January 2001

Preface

The original aerodrome at Aldergrove was born of wartime necessity. It was the scene of some of the early experiments in the development of civil aviation. It has been a base for all three of the fighting services in times of peace, war and civil strife. Record breakers and pioneers have completed or started their journeys on its runways.

As a civil airport, in 1963, it began on the crest of a wave of local pride, enthusiasm and confidence, sadly dampened by the years of terrorist activity which have blighted the life of the province. It has seen a number of changes of management, ownership and direction. It has faced and survived stiff competition from Belfast City and Dublin airports.

The future is now being welcomed with renewed confidence, in the hope of economic growth and renewed tourist potential in a peaceful environment. It has the great advantages of a long main runway; 24 hour operation; no noise abatement restrictions; the capacity to handle large volumes of scheduled passengers, charter traffic and freight; as well as the capacity to accept any size of aircraft currently in service. There is also plenty of room to expand the facilities when the need arises.

There are great challenges ahead – the marketplace for air travel, both in domestic and international terms, is tough and highly competitive.

The story of the last 80 years is both diverse and fascinating. There are few people in the country whose lives have not been touched in some way by the activities at Aldergrove, whether as travellers, employees, spectators or recipients of the morning newspaper or express parcel.

While civil operations have been given more weight in this account, this is not intended to minimise in any way the immense contribution made by the RAF, FAA or AAC at Aldergrove over the years. To tell the full story of the services' activities would require a book in itself. Perhaps other members of the Ulster Aviation Society will follow up this work and the 502 Squadron history *Flying the Red Hand* by the late Ron Parsons and Alan Watson, with a volume devoted to a detailed account of the regulars in peace and war.

Any readers encouraged by this book to take a deeper interest in aviation in Northern Ireland, past and present, are urged to join the Ulster Aviation Society – we are deeply indebted to our fellow members for their advice, help and archive material.

Finally, our grateful thanks are due to all of those who have given of their time and effort to make this project a reality; names, sources and references are listed in the acknowledgements and the bibliography. The commitment and enthusiasm shown by Paul Kehoe, from the time when the idea was first suggested to him, has been of immense importance. Our sincere apologies to any who have been inadvertently omitted.

Guy Warner
Jack Woods
Belfast
January 2001

Acknowledgements

Additional research by Gary Adams of the Ulster Aviation Society.

Correspondence with Sarah Able (British Midland); James Aiken (British Midland); Tony Brunskill (British Midland); Peter Clegg; Colin Cruddas; the Consultant Archivist Cobham plc; Julian Crow of KLM uk; Graham Day of Air Historical Branch MOD; Captain Bob Gardiner (British Midland); Fred Huntley MBE, the BA Consultant Archivist; Iain Hutchison; Roger Jackson; Tony Merton Jones of *Propliner* magazine and *Air Britain*; Captain Hayden Lawford (British Midland); Gerry Leslie (British Midland); Alan McFerran of the Modern Railway Society of Ireland; Simon Moody of the RAF Museum; Robert Nadin (British Midland); Mike Phipp; Eamon Power of Aer Lingus; John Stroud; and former Operations Director Doug Wilson.

Interviews: I Beattie, KB Boag, EC Body, K Duckett, W Eames, T Grant, J Hewitt, W Huston, D Jones, J Logan, A Keen, P Kehoe, WH McAlister, R McClune, R Martin, G Menary, A Moore, J Mulvany, J Murphy, Mrs M Phillips, A Silver, RG Spencer, D Warnock, G Willis and M Woodgate.

For assistance with illustrations, thanks are due to James Aitken, Stephen Boyd, Raymond Burrows, Peter Clegg, Peter Cooper, Ernie Cromie, Stephen Finny, Bob Gardiner, Ian Henderson, John Hewitt, Harry Holmes, Iain Hutchinson, Roger T Jackson, K Kelly, Hayden K Lawford, Tommy Maddock, Jim Logan, Peter Neill, Jack Patience, Brian Poots, Graham Simmons, RG Spencer, Mark Steenson and Les Thompson.

Grateful thanks are due to all the helpful members of staff in assisting with research at the Public Record Office for Northern Ireland, the Ulster Folk and Transport Museum, RAF Aldergrove, Donington Hall, Belfast City Hall and the Belfast City Library newspaper archives. At Belfast International Airport thanks are due to Paul Kehoe for his constant support and encouragement and to Uel Hoey, Cathy Kernan, Patricia McDonagh, Natalie Raper, Judith Steele and Esther Turtle. Thanks also to British Midland for flying me over to EMA. Special thanks for reading through the text to: Richard Cooke, Ernie Cromie, Noel Russell, Les Thompson (with his incredible eye for detail) and Bob Wilson.

Thanks also to Ronnie Hanna of Colourpoint Books for his very professional and thorough editing of the work; and to Barry Craig for his technical expertise in designing the page layout.

The work would not have been completed without Mrs Lynda Warner, whose support, tea and biscuits were much appreciated by her husband.

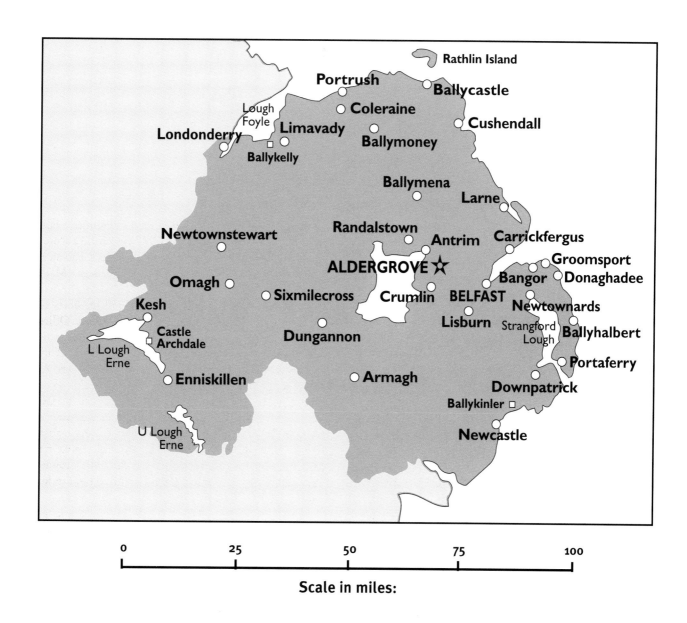

Northern Ireland showing principal places mentioned in the text.

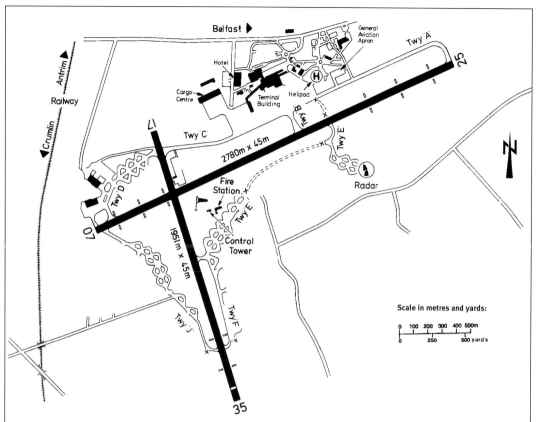

Belfast International Airport today (Belfast International Airport).

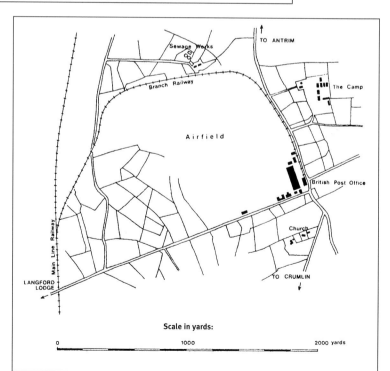

Aldergrove in 1920 (E Cromie).

Chapter 1

The First Decade

Beginnings

It was during 'Bloody April' 1917 that the Royal Flying Corps suffered substantial losses of pilots and aircraft, supporting General Haig's Arras offensive. It is ironic therefore that, only a few days into May, the youthful commanding officer of 43 Squadron, based at Triezennes in northern France, sustained serious injury when his Sopwith 1½ Strutter collided on take-off with a plough horse. While recuperating he was sent to Ireland, where his father was the Director of the National Gallery in Dublin. His mission was to survey likely sites for the establishment of airfields to accommodate the planned RFC expansion programme. His brief was to select eight fields with a clear take-off run of 500–600 yards in any direction. At that time there were no aerodromes in Ireland, so he flew his BE2c by way of Stranraer in Scotland, to Larne and then south to Dublin, where he landed in Phoenix Park. Two of the fields which he chose subsequently became Dublin Airport at Collinstown and Casement Aerodrome, Baldonnel – the home of the Irish Air Corps.

A third was in the north – 170 acres of farmland, 16 miles west of Belfast, close to Lough Neagh and the village of Crumlin, in the townlands of Ballyquillan, Seacash,

Major Sholto Douglas.   *J Woods Collection*

British and Ballyrobin, which all lay within the parish of Killead. The area had been inhabited for several thousand years, since the first mesolithic hunter-gatherers had made their way along the Upper Bann to the shores of the lough. Later evidence of settlement was the numerous bronze age raths, the earthen remains of homesteads. The parish then came to form part of the demesne of Sir Neill O'Neill, who forfeited his lands to Queen Elizabeth, following which they were sold at auction by the government in Dublin. Local tradition maintains that the land was heavily forested until the beginning of the eighteenth century. About 150 years later it was prosperous farmland, devoted to the growing of wheat, oats and potatoes. About one third of the parish was owned by the Pakenham family, whose residence was Langford Lodge. Overall the parish had an "aspect of richness"[1], noted by the writer of the Ordnance Survey report of 1833. Killead girls were known for their beauty, while the men were famed for their longevity – any connection between these attributes is not recorded.

The site was purchased by the Air Ministry in 1917. The farmland became Aldergrove and the airman who chose it was Sholto Douglas, later to become a peer of the realm, a Marshal of the Royal Air Force and chairman of British European Airways.

Royal Aircraft Factory BE2c.   *J Woods Collection*

Aircraft Construction

Frederick Handley Page built his first aeroplane in 1910. By 1917, Handley Page O/100 and O/400 twin-engine heavy bombers were being produced in quantity for the Royal Flying Corps and Royal Naval Air Service. In August of that year the war cabinet authorised the construction of three prototypes of an even larger machine. As the Handley Page (HP) factory in Cricklewood in north London was working to full capacity, it was decided to make use of the expert draughtsmen, carpenters and fitters of the shipbuilders Harland and Wolff Ltd, in Belfast. To this end, the Chief Designer, GR Volkert, went there to take charge of the project at the head of a team from HP, while Frederick Handley Page himself visited the city every weekend to monitor progress (returning to London by means of the Larne–Stranraer ferry *Princess Maud* on Mondays, with all the Ulster ham and bacon he could carry).

Harland and Wolff already had relevant experience in aircraft manufacture, having commenced in 1916 the construction of an eventual total of nearly 1,000 single-engine DH6s and Avro 504s, which were shipped by water to England.

On 28 February 1918 Aldergrove was selected as the site for the flying test field, with the result that the construction of final assembly hangars was needed. Because of delays by the building contractors, the flight sheds were not ready in time for the first prototype – though to be fair, when completed, Aldergrove had one of the largest hangars in the British Isles, measuring over 500 feet long. So the massive HP V/1500, with its four Rolls Royce Eagle engines, was transported in parts to Cricklewood (the fuselage was shipped directly to London but the wings went by way of the *Princess Maud* from Larne and then by rail to Euston), where it flew for the first time, registered as B9463, on 22 May 1918.

Present when the aerodrome was opened that autumn was Margaret Nelson, aged 11. Eighty years later, as Mrs Margaret Phillips, she remembers the massive building, far larger than her father's barn, crowded with guests. A good number of local people were invited to a buffet lunch "with plenty of cakes and cream and biscuits and lemonade"[2]. Margaret was one of the few children present, as her cousin, Philip Gillan, was one of the farmers, along with Messrs McCaffrey, Arbuckle, Thompson and Molyneaux (the grandfather of Lord Molyneaux), who had sold their land to the Air Ministry. A single aircraft, probably an Avro, graced the new concrete apron. Some days later, while working in the field haymaking, Margaret saw two small biplanes from Aldergrove buzzing above, one of which thrilled her by looping the loop. Some of her sense of wonder may be gained from the fact that any form of mechanised transport in the locality was a rarity, bicycle or horse and cart being the norm.

Access to the aerodrome was further improved by the construction of a branch line from the main Belfast to Antrim railway, which ran around the north side of the airfield to a point near Killead.

The first V/1500 to fly from Aldergrove (now No 16 Aircraft Acceptance Park) was E4307, which took to the air on 20 December 1918 in the experienced hands of Clifford Prodger, HP's 28-year-old American test pilot. As described by the *Belfast Telegraph*, he was "on a circular tour, passing over Divis Mountain. At two o'clock the aeroplane was right over the city and was an object of intense curiosity, the observers including thousands of mill hands and office workers."[3] The aircraft was entirely satisfactory and departed for England the next day, to be followed by E4308 on 18 January 1919, with a crew of seven, and half a ton of freight on board.

The *Belfast Telegraph* was also most impressed by the pilot, describing Clifford Prodger in the following terms: "If you can visualise the features of a man, little more than a youth, of middle height, firm chin and an alien to affectation, you have a portrait of a hero of a thousand flights over England, Ireland, Scotland, Wales and France."[4] The aircraft was equally striking: "At Aldergrove, the great machine could be viewed in all its majesty and massiveness. The opportunity of an internal inspection was availed of with obvious avidity. There was no suggestion of discomfort or space limitation, it being so lofty and so roomy that all parts from nose to tail are accessible."[5]

Three more aircraft were added in May, all flown by Clifford Prodger (who sadly was killed the following year when his aircraft dived into the ground at Redwood, California), but the Armistice had ended the need for large numbers of an aeroplane specifically designed to bomb Germany. The last fully documented Harland and Wolff-built V/1500 was J6573, which was powered by Napier Lions and was flown from Aldergrove by Major Keith Park on 3 September 1919. However, it appears that two further V/1500s, piloted by Park again and none other than Wing Commander Sholto Douglas, departed from Aldergrove in June 1920. He later described the V/1500 thus:

As was the custom with nearly all of these early aircraft, the pilot sat in an open cockpit behind a

Handley Page V/1500 E4307 at Aldergrove, 20 December 1918.   *Ulster Folk and Transport Museum*

large windscreen with a great wheel in front of him for the controls. There were no engine instruments in the cockpit. They were mounted on panels on the frames between the wings holding the radiators of the engines and the pilot could only just see them through the whirling disks of the propellers. Petrol from the two-thousand gallon fuel tank in the body of the aircraft was fed to the four engines by wind-driven pumps. It was always surprising to me how well the engines stood up to the caning we gave them. When we opened up the throttles to take off there was no easing them back after we were airborne. We left them there at full power as we needed all that we could get out of the engines to keep going. Part of the tool kit was some chewing gum and insulating tape for quick repairs to the water jackets of those engines. They always seemed to be springing leaks and the gum was chewed and then plugged in the leak and secured with the tape.[6]

The V/1500 was a masterpiece of contemporary technology, weighing 13$\frac{1}{2}$ tons. It had a wingspan of 126'0", a fuselage length of 64'0", carried a crew of six and was capable of carrying 7,500 lbs of bombs 1,300 miles. It had an endurance of 17 hours in the air and had a top speed of 99 mph. Its four undercarriage wheels were each 5'0" in

diameter. The aircraft's lifting capacity was well tested on 15 November 1918 at Cricklewood, when a party of 28 journalists was invited aloft by Frederick Handley Page, as well as 12 employees. In all, 40 passengers were taken to 6,500 feet for a joyride over London.

Belfast, Harland and Wolff and Aldergrove can be proud of their contribution to the first British 'Jumbo'.

Post-war Service Use

Keith Park's association with Aldergrove was not confined to the V/1500. The New Zealand-born ace – who scored 20 kills flying the Bristol Fighter with 48 Squadron on the Western Front, and as an Air Vice Marshal was the steely commander of 11 Group in the Battle of Britain – carried out a remarkable endurance flight in an O/400 in April 1919. Flying F3750 *Last Days* of No1 Air Navigation and Bombing School, he circumnavigated the British Isles. The flight began from Andover in Hampshire. The first leg followed the east coast route to Edinburgh, the next day rounding the north of Scotland and heading down the west coast for the sea crossing to Aldergrove. When they arrived, the airfield was fog-bound, it was 7.00 pm and the fuel was running low. Park completed a masterly feat of airmanship by bringing off a crosswind landing at Queen's Island on a Harland and Wolff wharf which measured only 400 yards by 50 yards. The rest of the crew went to Aldergrove by road. Park took off the next morning, picked them up and continued the circuit via Dublin, Pembroke, Bodmin, Plymouth and Bournemouth, returning to Andover after four days, by which time the aircraft had covered 1,600 miles in 30 hours in the air.

'Ulster's Great Aerodrome'

In May 1919, a regular columnist for the *Northern Whig*, who wrote under the pseudonym 'An Old Fogey' wrote an article entitled 'Ulster's Great Aerodrome'. He was moved to quote Lord Tennyson, who foresaw "the nation's airy navies grappling in the central blue", which had certainly been realised in the preceding four years, but he also looked forward to another of his lordship's predictions coming to pass: "...the heavens filled with commerce, argosies with magic sails, pilots of the purple twilight, dropping down with costly bales"[7].

The 'Old Fogey' described his visit to Aldergrove:

"Straight on and about a mile ahead, you'll come right on to the 'drum. You can see it from the railway bridge." I followed the direction indicated by the farmer and, sure enough, from the top of the bridge, I saw ahead a bulky building close to the road. And as I approached, I had ample evidence that the building was Aldergrove Aerodrome, known locally as "the 'drum". A graceful Avro shot up suddenly from the enclosure into the air and soon, notwithstanding that a stiff gale was blowing from Lough Neagh, the daring RAF pilot was executing right overhead the most astounding manoeuvres. Watching the performance, I could not help recalling the first flying exhibition in Ireland, held at Leopardstown only eight years ago. How the aviation heroes of that day – Drexel with his Bleriot and Grace with his Farman, would have stared with wonder at this unknown pilot of today, with his Avro and his amazing stunts.

But the familiarity which breeds indifference was strikingly exemplified in the demeanour of the local labourers who were sweeping the road in front of the " 'drum". Stolidly they continued their occupation, lifting not a glance of either appreciation or apprehension towards the Avro.

For nearly two years, a small army of workmen has been engaged in construction work. Hundreds still remain and are busy there daily. It will be well into summer before "finis" can be written upon the finest

concern of its kind in Ireland. The place has cost already – so it is said – a cool half million. It is worth it as the only permanent aerodrome in Ulster. And it is an establishment which will, without doubt, be essential in view of the developments in aerial activity both for national defence and postal and passenger purposes, which are inevitable in the near future.[8]

The writer went on to describe the site:

The land was drained, levelled where necessary and the "park" portion was sown with grass-seed, after which the buildings were proceeded with. These have been erected by Messrs. M'Laughlin & Harvey. The central aeroplane shed holds half a dozen of the largest type of machine besides a number of the smaller types such as the Avros. Another shed in course of construction will accommodate about seven or eight more. It was intended by Messrs. Harland & Wolff to have 120 to 150 skilled workmen resident on the premises. For these as well as for the administration department of the RAF excellent provision is made. All the buildings when completed will be taken over by the Air Ministry, to whom the entire property belongs. The camp of the RAF detachment is situated about a quarter of a mile from the aerodrome buildings. Here too the buildings are of a solid and permanent character with stonefaced brickwork. There is a first class wireless telegraphy installation and of course electric lighting and inter-telephone systems to every department. The premises which are about a mile from Aldergrove Station on the Lisburn and Antrim branch of the G.N.R. are connected with that line by a siding which runs right into the drome. Captain Workman M.C. is the officer in charge of the Acceptance Park for the RAF.[9]

There then followed a speculative section entitled 'Commercial Flying':

Now the Air Ministry have published a map showing the several routes for the guidance of pilots and have issued a set of rules of the road and a scale of the charges to be made for the accommodation of civil aviators and their machines at government aerodromes including Aldergrove. At the same time yesterday morning's newspapers record how a Handley Page aeroplane flew on Thursday from London to Manchester carrying ten passengers and some hundredweights of luggage. [*This flight was undertaken on 1 May from Cricklewood to Alexandra Park in the O/400 D8350 of Handley Page Transport*

– piloted by Sholto Douglas, who had temporarily left the RAF to become chief pilot of this early airline.] Transatlantic commercial flying in the opinion of experienced aviators will come in the near future and the importance of Aldergrove may be still further enhanced by its becoming an important Transatlantic air station. Then we may expect announcements in our Saturday morning newspaper such as the following – "Belfast and New York Air Service – Departures from Aldergrove next week as follows: Thursday, "Dalriada" 3000 hp: Saturday "Ben Madigan" 4000 hp: both Belfast built airships. For passage apply etc."[10]

There is no doubt that Aldergrove made a favourable impression and that its potential was recognised. Indeed the Air Ministry's Department of Civil Aviation in London acknowledged this also. A plan of a possible nation-wide air route system, issued in 1919, designated Aldergrove as the civil air terminus on the route north from Hounslow via Hucknall, Didsbury, Scale Hall and Luce Bay. This scheme did not progress beyond the pipe-dream stage and so Aldergrove's destiny was not to be realised in full until some 44 years later.

The Civil War Period

The reason for the existence of No16 Air Acceptance Park may have ceased, but Aldergrove was kept available

and a flight of Bristol Fighters from 4 Squadron Royal Air Force (as the RFC and RNAS had become on 1 April 1918) was stationed there from 1920 to 1922. Communications with 11 Group Headquarters were maintained by the DH9s and Bristol Fighters of 100 Squadron based at Baldonnel. With the signing of the Anglo-Irish Treaty, the RAF began the process of withdrawal from what was now the Irish Free State in 1922. However, with the probability of civil war between the supporters and opponents of the Treaty looming, it was decided to retain the Irish Flight of four Bristol Fighters at Baldonnel to protect the evacuation of British forces.

On 31 May 1922, 2 Squadron was moved from England to Aldergrove. A detailed report on the first week of activities at their new base, signed by Wing Commander AV Bettington, Commanding RAF Ulster, has survived. Twelve Bristol Fighters were dispatched from RAF Digby and flew via Collinstown to Aldergrove. "Mechanical transport laden with stores, consisting of four heavy tenders, one workshop tender, five light tenders, one ambulance, one Hucks starter, one touring car and three motor cycles and side-cars"[11] proceeded in convoy to Holyhead and thence by sea to Belfast. "The remainder of the personnel, 12 officers and 97 airmen under Squadron Leader L.F. Forbes MC, commanding the squadron",[12] embarked at Fleetwood. To begin with, flying was restricted by a lack of petrol and oil. However, aerial reconnaissance

The de Havilland DH9c which staged through Aldergrove on 1 July 1922.   *HK Lawford Collection*

of several proposed landing grounds in Fermanagh, near Omagh, Newtownards, Ballykinler and Orangefield in Belfast took place. The squadron's principal tasks were defined as "the establishment of an aerial mail between Belfast and Dublin and preparations to co-operate with various brigades and patrols along the Ulster border".[13]

The mail service between Collinstown and Aldergrove began on 7 June and was flown at a rate of up to two aircraft a day until 23 October. Aircraft from 2 Squadron and the Irish Flight were used. The mails were carried by an army courier, who was under strict instructions to destroy confidential material in the event of a forced landing. The aeroplanes' machine guns were either removed or rendered inoperable for flights over Irish territory. With the outbreak of hostilities in the Free State at the end of June, a detachment of 2 Squadron aircraft was maintained at Collinstown, fully armed with bombs and ready to act if required. The newsreel companies and newspapers were anxious to cover the strife and while most flew directly to Dublin, there is evidence that one DH9c, G-EBCZ of the de Havilland Aeroplane Hire Service, staged through Aldergrove on 1 July and was escorted south on two occasions by a Bristol Fighter.

The mail service was not without incident, as four aircraft had to make forced landings en route, while on 9 October the first recorded ditching of an aircraft in Lough Neagh took place, when a Bristol Fighter, J6705 of 2 Squadron, landed in the water after suffering an engine failure. Both of the crew members were rescued by fishing boat after 40 uncomfortable minutes in the water. The pilot was only slightly injured but the passenger, Wing Commander Bettington, suffered a broken jaw. Three months earlier the senior RAF officer in Ireland, Group Captain I Bonham Carter, had also made a premature descent near Downpatrick on his way to Aldergrove in his personal BE2c C6977. The final withdrawal began in November, with aircraft, men and material being brought from Collinstown to Aldergrove. At the same time 2 Squadron also prepared to leave, with the move to Farnborough beginning at the end of December. By February 1923 all the Bristol Fighters had departed and the airfield was placed under care and maintenance.

Early Civil Flights

Meanwhile, on 22 June 1921, King George V and Queen Mary visited Northern Ireland in the royal yacht, to open the new parliament. *Flight* magazine heralded the aviation aspects of the visit: "Yet once again the aeroplane

has given popular demonstration of its capabilities of playing an extremely important part in modern commerce... aeroplanes were employed, with the most satisfactory results, by the press and a cinematograph firm for the purpose of conveying photographs and other important matter between London and Belfast and back".[14]

Two DH9s arrived on behalf of *The Times*, Pathe Freres and the *Daily Graphic*. Both were supplied for charter, at a rate of two shillings (10p) a mile, through Captain DM Greig of the Air Express Company. One was piloted by Alan Cobham and the other by FW Hatchett. The DH4A G-EAMU *City of York* of the Instone Air Line Ltd, was flown in by Captain FL Barnard (who would later become Imperial Airways' chief pilot) for the *Daily Mail* and the *Daily Mirror*. An Avro 548 G-EAPQ with its owner, Captain EDC Hearne, acting for the *Daily Sketch*, with AO Russell of Aero Films Ltd as his passenger, completed the aerial activity. The Avro was a conversion of the famous 504 and in 1920–21 completed a photographic survey of the whole of England, the entire coastline of Belgium and France and the major Belgian inland towns. Alan Cobham, having crossed the coast at Donaghadee, made a somewhat risky initial descent into "a field at Balmoral where an aeroplane had once landed"[15] and unloaded a consignment of that morning's edition of *The Times*, before proceeding to Aldergrove where all the aeroplanes were serviced and refuelled. Film and still photographs were taken of their Majesties' arrival at Donegall Quay and motorcade to the City Hall and rushed to the waiting aircraft, which had all departed again before 2 o'clock.

The return journey was not without incident, as Hatchett had to make a forced landing and transfer the films to Cobham's aircraft. While this was being effected, Captain Barnard roared overhead at high speed, which he estimated at up to 200 mph, which implied a considerable tailwind. The three remaining aircraft all reached their destinations by teatime – Cricklewood for the DH9, Croydon for the DH4 and Hendon for the Avro. Pathe were able to show a film of the event in London cinemas that evening, while the national newspapers included photographs of the principal parts of the ceremony the following morning. The *Belfast Newsletter* saw this enterprise as "another illustration of the remarkable strides made in rapid transit".[16]

The closing days of 1922 saw an early experiment in the creation of a global media village, when a special Ulster edition of *The Times* (which reviewed the province's economic and political developments after the first year of the local parliament) was flown from Chester to Aldergrove

The de Havilland DH4A that visited Aldergrove on 22 June 1921.   *AJ Jackson*

on the day of publication, 5 December. The aircraft involved were two DH16s of the de Havilland Aeroplane Hire Service – G-EALM and G-EAPT, flown by Captain CD Barnard and HS Broad. A Bristol Fighter was dispatched from Aldergrove at 11.00 am to guide the visitors and to allow a photographer from *The Times* the opportunity to take some aerial views of Belfast. At 11.30 am, the two de Havillands came in sight and landed a few minutes later. The pilots commented that it been a rough passage, with the wind blowing a gale. After the papers were unloaded and sent on their way in Easons' vans, there followed a ceremonial exchange of civic greetings, before the two doubtless hungry pilots were "entertained to refreshments by Lieut Colonel Pakenham of Langford Lodge".[17] One aircraft made the return journey before dusk the same afternoon. The other was flown to Dublin by Hubert Broad the following day, escorted by three Bristol Fighters, and returned to England via Phoenix Park – so ending the flying activities of the RAF in Eire. Hubert Broad later became de Havilland's chief test pilot, while Captain Barnard became personal pilot to the Duchess of Bedford.

The DH4s and DH9s were fairly basic conversions of wartime light bombers, adapted to carry one or two passengers. The DH16, while based on the same airframe, was designed with an enclosed passenger cabin covered by a hinged, glazed canopy and could accommodate 800 lbs of cargo or four people in relative, if cramped, comfort.

Early Passenger Services

The first passenger schedules to Northern Ireland were of brief duration. On 15 September 1923 Alan Cobham, in the prototype DH50 G-EBFN, flew the first of a short series of flights linking Plymouth, Birmingham, Manchester and Belfast (Aldergrove). The main object was the rapid conveyance of the incoming American mails, particularly those in respect of the linen trade. There was great rivalry for a share of the important American market between linen makers in the north of England, Northern Ireland and those in northern France. It was conceived that the mail service would allow the British producers a time advantage over their competitors. A few passengers were also flown, including the Mayor of Plymouth, Mr Solomon Stephens, and his daughter, Laura, as well as civic gifts of Devonshire cream. In return Mr Stephens was presented with a blackthorn stick.

Laura Stephens had merely turned up in Plymouth with her father to wave off the aeroplane, but on hearing that there was a vacant seat, persuaded him to let her go as far as Birmingham. Once on board, she enjoyed the experience so much that she was reluctant to give up her seat, telling the *Belfast Telegraph* in an article entitled 'Flying Over the Rainbow', "They wanted me to leave at Birmingham and again at Manchester but I wouldn't miss the trip for anything. I liked the trip across the sea and it was great to look down on Belfast. I saw some boys playing cricket in a field. I was not in the least bit upset and was most

De Havilland DH50.   *PT Capon*

comfortable. It was just delicious."[18] When flying over Belfast, she leaned out the window to view the sights of the city, the 100 mph slipstream playing havoc with her hair,: "It was all knotted up and I could hardly get it fixed in time to look presentable when I landed."[19]

The Lord Mayor of Belfast, Alderman WG Turner, also took to the air for a pleasure flight "over part of Lough Neagh, Crumlin, the Cavehill, Belfast and Belfast Lough",[20] thus becoming the first airborne alderman of the city. He enjoyed his trip: "I was not a bit nervous. The sun was shining brightly on Lough Neagh, which looked very pretty. The fields seemed about the size of postage stamps. We were not far above the Cavehill and Mr.Cobham said that we flew over Belfast at the rate of 130 miles an hour. We were 3000 feet up, it was very comfortable and very pleasant."[21] Alan Cobham commented that after his short joy-flight, the Lord Mayor "became a convert to the flying game and convinced that Belfast must develop into an air port".[22] A daily service (excluding Sundays) was maintained until 4 October.

Newspapers were also flown from Manchester, using the DH9c G-EBAX, during the same period, with the specially marked vans of Eason's Motor Service 'By Air To-Day', meeting the aeroplane at Aldergrove, where a ton of papers was unloaded for "despatch to all parts of Ulster".[23] It is known that these flights took place on 27, 28 and 29 September and 2 October. On one occasion at least, the pilot was Captain Walter Hope of the DH Aeroplane Hire Service. On 16 October 1923, the process was reversed,

with the Belfast newspaper, the *Northern Whig* being sent to Manchester as "the first Irish newspaper to try the experiment".[24]

An alternative to Aldergrove was Malone Air Park on the southern outskirts of Belfast. It was an ambitious project, financed to the tune of £15,000 by the City Corporation. The first commercial flight from Malone was made by Alan Cobham on 30 April 1924 in the DH50 G-EBFP to Liverpool, Aintree. However, the sodden state of the ground that day, which rendered take-off more difficult, was a portent of the troubles facing this venture. The primary aim was to deliver London newspapers to Northern Ireland more speedily than before. However, on the return flight to Liverpool passengers could be carried.

As well as the problems with the Malone site, the weather was often unkind and diversions to Aldergrove were frequent. Northern Airlines tried other routes, from Glasgow in June and Carlisle in September. Then in March 1925, a daily service to Stranraer began, which lasted nearly three months. Newspapers were sent to Scotland by air, the first instance being on 23 March and involving the *Belfast Telegraph*. The aircraft used by Northern Airlines were the DH9s G-EBJW and G-EBJX, as well as the more powerful four-seat DH50s G-EBFN and 'FP.

The last straw was the experience of RH McIntosh, 'All-Weather Mac' (so-called after landing at a fogbound Croydon in the HP O/10 G-EATH on 20 October 1921), on 14 April 1925. He was on six months unpaid leave from Imperial Airways and was temporarily appointed as

Left: De Havilland DH9c G-EBAX delivering the mail to Easons.

Easons

Above: De Havilland
DH9 G-EBJW of
Northern Airlines.
WJ Halland

Right: De Havilland
DH9 G-EBJX of
Northern Airlines.
AJ Jackson

Northern Airlines' chief pilot. On making a difficult landing at Malone in a hailstorm, the machine was lifted by a gust of wind and tossed 50 feet into a hedge, luckily without severe damage. The distinguished and experienced pilot later claimed that it was the worst route for bad weather he had encountered. McIntosh served in both world wars, with the RFC and then the RAF, and in 45 years of flying he eventually logged the immense total of 23,000 hours in 143 different types of aircraft – so his opinion was given with some authority. Soon the Air Ministry equipment at Malone was transferred to Aldergrove. By June, Northern Airlines' bold unsubsidised venture was over. Nearly a decade was to pass before a regular air service would link Northern Ireland with the mainland.

The de Havilland aircraft were all single-engine biplanes. Bearing in mind the fairly fragile wood and fabric structure of the aircraft, the distinct possibility of engine failure, the rudimentary meteorological advice available and the lack of navigational or radio facilities, the sea crossing from England or Scotland to Northern Ireland was not without hazard. The courage and fortitude of those early pioneers and any intrepid passengers should not be underestimated. The pilot was exposed to the elements in the open cockpit, protected by a leather helmet, goggles, gauntlets and a full length heavy leather coat. Travellers boarded the aircraft by climbing onto the lower wing from the rear and then clambered through the glazed, hinged hatch into the passenger compartment. In the DH50 there was room for four in the snug cabin which lay between the engine and the pilot. A graphic account of a flight in a DH50 in 1923 was written for the *Belfast Telegraph* by Major Blake, the air correspondent of the *Daily News*:

> Two machines, a DH50 and a DH9c, left Belfast together, the former piloted by Mr. Alan Cobham and the other by Captain Hope. The DH9c cut straight over the sea from Ireland to Lancashire and did the journey in one hour and fifty-five minutes, whilst we took the safer route [along] the coast and accomplished the trip in ten minutes more. It was raining slightly and the sky was full of heavy clouds when we left Aldergrove aerodrome. The machine was being bumped all over the place. One violent drop brought the 'plane up with a jerk, throwing the water bottle up in the cabin out of its socket and jolting the passengers' heads against the ceiling. Over the Irish sea we were unable to get up 1000 feet in the air on account of the dense clouds, while below the sea was churned into froth by a high wind. We skirted the coast of the Solway Firth gradually being

driven lower and lower by storm clouds until we were racing along the seashore little more than 100 feet from the ground. All the time we were being violently bumped and time after time, the pilot had to make a detour in order to avoid a heavier storm than usual. Over Lancashire, we were flying through heavy rain with black clouds brushing the top of the machine, skirting the tree tops and dodging factory chimneys. Horses in the fields bolted as we thundered overhead at a speed of 130 miles an hour, while hedge, factories and villages went by in one continuous stream. Near Preston, we had to climb into the clouds to avoid the factory chimneys as we came down for Didsbury aerodrome. It was not a pleasant trip but the thing that mattered had been achieved, the mails got through on time. My admiration for the DH50 grows greater daily. She is wonderfully steady in heavy weather and passengers are well-protected from draught and rain, without the cabin being stuffy.[25]

A more bibulous occasion with the Lord Mayor of Belfast is recounted in Alan Cobham's early book of memoirs, *Skyways*:

> They were very jolly passengers and I was highly amused when I looked through the window from the pilot's cockpit to the cabin to see that the Lord Mayor had turned the shelf in the front of the cabin into a miniature cocktail bar and was busy administering liberal doses of a famous extract into several glasses. After handing drinks to Sir Sefton Brancker and the journalists on board, he then prepared one for me but was prevented from handing it through the cockpit window by the Director of Civil Aviation, who said it was against the rules for the pilot to drink during flight. The cockpit window was open and the odours that wafted through told me that it was a good brand.[26]

Alan Cobham's involvement with the early years at Aldergrove is worthy of note as he was one of the most famous figures in British aviation in the years between the two world wars. Following service with the RFC and RAF he worked for the de Havilland company and then, in 1924, he made the first of his great survey flights which explored the feasibility of what were later to become Imperial Airways' Empire Air Routes. He flew to Rangoon in 1924, to Cape Town in 1926 and later in the same year to Australia (for which feat he received his knighthood).

From 502 to WW2

502 motto, 'I fear nothing'.

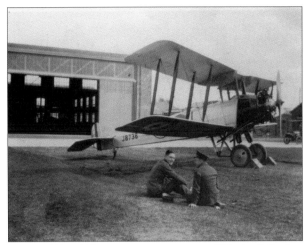

Avro 504N at Aldergrove.   *J Hewitt Collection*

Enter 502 Squadron

The military role of Aldergrove received an enormous boost in May 1925 with the initial formation of 502 (Ulster) Bombing Squadron. The previous year the Air Ministry had approved the creation of Special Reserve Squadrons and the first of these was 502. The aim was to increase the combat strength of the RAF with local part-time volunteers augmenting a nucleus of regular personnel, who would enlist and instruct the reservists. The creation of this 'yeomanry of the air' was principally due to the foresight and drive of Marshal of the RAF Lord Trenchard. The new squadron occupied the hangars and buildings formerly used by No 16 AAP and a recruiting office in Belfast was opened in July. The first aircraft on strength

were Avro 504 twin-seat biplane trainers and the much larger Vickers Vimy twin-engine bombers. Neither type was in the first flush of youth – the Avro 504 dated from 1913, while the Vimy had made its maiden flight in 1917. Both, however, were justly famous – the 504 as one of the greatest training aircraft of all time; and the Vimy was the type which had carried Captain John Alcock and Lieutenant Arthur Whitten Brown across the Atlantic from St John's, Newfoundland, to Derrygimbla Bog, near Clifden in County Galway, on 14–15 June 1919.

Proof of 502 Squadron's growing competence was given on 25 March 1926 when, led by the Commanding Officer, Squadron Leader RD Oxland, a flight by four aircraft was made around Ulster, carrying members of the press and with the aim of encouraging recruiting. The *Belfast Telegraph* reported the event as follows:

> Round Ulster in three and a half hours! A few years ago this would have sounded ridiculous...On arrival at the aerodrome, the press representatives who took part in the flight were supplied with suitable flying costumes...the engines were started and the pilots and mechanics took their places and in a few minutes we were taxiing across the aerodrome. On reaching

Vickers Vimy over Co Down.   *J Hewitt Collection*

the distant side the machines and, engines opened out, we were racing across the grass and in a second or two rose smoothly into the air. After circling around the shores of Lough Neagh for about fifteen minutes, the machines got into formation and headed straight for Belfast, the time being 10.40...Belfast was reached at 10.55. The shipyards showed up particularly well...In ten minutes time Bangor was reached...we headed south down the Ards Peninsula passing over Newtownards and Downpatrick...we proceeded along the coast to Newcastle, where we passed right over the town. The Mourne Mountains were absolutely fog bound and we could only just trace their outline. We then turned sharply inland and steered for Armagh. Here the Roman Catholic Cathedral showed up remarkably well. We continued our flight over County Tyrone, passing over Dungannon, Sixmilecross and Omagh. We then crossed into County Fermanagh, the journey here being principally over bogland...From Enniskillen we headed towards Newtownstewart and followed the River Foyle to a point near Derry, turning eastwards we passed over Limavady and were soon near Coleraine. This part of the trip was very attractive, the panoramic view of mountains and moorland with their varying tints of colour being exceedingly

beautiful. We followed the course of the River Bann to Lough Neagh and continued over Randalstown and Antrim. Next we commenced a gradual descent and reached terra firma at Aldergrove again after three and a half hours in the air. Our average height was 2000 feet, which was considerably increased when passing over the mountains. As well as the C.O., the other pilots were Flight Lieutenant Toogood, Flying Officer M'Kinlay Hay and Flying Officer Hall. Altogether the trip was most enjoyable although somewhat bumpy especially over North Derry.[27]

Two months later, the squadron was authorised to use the 'Red Hand of Ulster' as the symbol on its badge and aircraft.

Another important development at Aldergrove in July 1926 was the setting up of a civilian meteorological unit under the direction of JD Ashton and his staff of three.

The robust and reliable Vimy served with the squadron until 1928, when it was replaced by the Handley Page Hyderabad, the last heavy bomber of wooden construction to serve with the RAF. Forty-five of this type were produced, which had a direct ancestry back to the O/400s and V/1500s of a decade earlier. The Hyderabad is thought

Vickers Vimy with 502 Squadron symbol.

J Hewitt Collection

Handley Page Hyderabad during exercise on Tyrella beach,
Co Down.   *J Hewitt Collection*

to be unique in RAF service in that not a single fatality was suffered by those flying it.

On 13 July 1928 five Avro 504Ns belonging to the squadron took part in the first air race in Ulster, held at Bangor, as part of the Royal Ulster Yacht Club Regatta. This event, which was run over two laps of an eleven mile triangular course, helped promote growing aviation awareness in the province. This was further emphasised by the formation of the North of Ireland Aero Club at the Grand Central Hotel, Belfast on 28 September.

At about this time a local boatman, Henry McGarry, was engaged to look after a number of canvas targets which were placed in Lough Neagh to facilitate bombing practice. From this modest start, over the following decade, rather more comprehensive range facilities would be developed.

In August 1929 the Avro 504K G-EBXA of the North British Aviation Company landed at Aldergrove. The pilot was Captain EE Fresson, who was later to found Highland Airways and develop air services to Orkney and Shetland from Inverness. His purpose in Ulster was to provide pleasure flying from Groomsport and Dundonald, taking advantage of the crowds provided by the TT races.

The innate conservatism of British aircraft design in this period is well shown by the Hyderabad's successor, the Vickers Virginia, which joined 502 Squadron in the winter of 1931–32. The internal structure of the aircraft may have been all-metal, but it was still fabric-covered, a biplane, with the crew open to the elements and having an optimistic top speed of 108 mph.

As the aircraft changed, the infrastructure was improved too, with the construction of Officers' and Sergeants' messes, airmen's married quarters and hangars.

Vickers Virginia of 502 Squadron.

J Hewitt Collection

Famous Personalities

On 22 May 1932 a very famous personality landed at Aldergrove – the great aviator Amelia Earhart. The previous day she had completed the first female solo crossing of the Atlantic from Harbour Grace, Newfoundland to Culmore, County Londonderry in her Lockheed Vega. She transferred to a Desoutter air-taxi of National Flying Services and was taken onwards to London via Blackpool, to be followed by her aircraft a few days afterwards (it being taken by road to Belfast and then shipped to England).

Later the same year, on 16 November, the Prince of Wales opened the new parliament buildings at Stormont. A formation of five 502 Squadron Vickers Virginias took off from Aldergrove and dipped their wings in salute as the Prince arrived at Donegall Quay.

Then, on 2 July 1933, 24 Savoia Marchetti S55x flying boats of the Italian Air Force, under the command of General Italo Balbo, landed on Lough Foyle en route to Chicago and the first crossing in formation of the North Atlantic. The following day the Secretary of State for Air, Lord Londonderry, arrived at Aldergrove from London in a Hawker Hart of 24 Squadron RAF. From there he was conveyed to Lough Neagh, where he boarded a Supermarine Southampton flying boat of 201 Squadron, in which he flew to Lough Foyle to greet General Balbo.

The Air Display of 1933

The first civil air display in the north since that held at the Balmoral Showgrounds, Belfast, in 1912, took place at Aldergrove on 1 July 1933. It proved to be highly popular and included pleasure flying in the Avro Ten G-ACGF, de Havilland Dragon G-ACDL and DH 83 Fox Moth G-ACCT of Midland and Scottish Air Ferries. The Dragon was also used to carry out the day's scheduled services to Campbeltown and Glasgow (of which more later), while the Fox Moth's first task was to collect Lord Londonderry and family. Service participation was provided by 502 Squadron and by Westland Wapitis from 602 Squadron, based at Renfrew. Several notable aviators of the time visited with their own aircraft, including a Percival Gull, GA Monospar and DH Puss Moth, Fox Moth and Gipsy Moth. Other attractions included aerial balloon bursting by some of these visitors and a parachute jump by Mr A Gilmour, who the *Northern Whig* reported "made a perfect landing on the road just outside the aerodrome".[27]

A highly unusual type taking part was the Cierva autogyro G-ABUC, piloted by AC Rowson. This was in essence the fuselage of an aircraft without wings, but fitted instead with a three-bladed rotor mounted above. It was not a true helicopter, as the rotors were not driven by the engine, but it had a spectacular short take-off and landing capability. It was also capable of very slow flying by virtue of its stalling speed of only 20 mph.

Aldergrove's first civil air display, July 1933. *RAF Aldergrove*

Interest in aviation was further raised by the visits to the lately reclaimed land at Sydenham in 1933, and subsequently to Newtownards in 1935, of Sir Alan Cobham's National Aviation Day Displays (which included HP W10 G-EBMM, HP 33 Clive III G-ABYX, DH83 Fox Moth G-ACEY, Airspeed Ferry G-ABSI and Avro 504 G-ABVH). These events offered joy rides and spectacular stunts, as part of a tour which took in Waterford, Clonmel, Cork, Limerick, Oranmore (Galway), Bundoran, Londonderry, Portrush, Enniskillen, Dublin and Dundalk. Interestingly, Alan Cobham bought the 16-seat Clive following the abandonment by the Air Council of a scheme to use the aircraft for a London to Belfast passenger service.

One of the first recorded landings at Sydenham had been on 31 May 1933 by Colonel the Master of Sempill, a well known airman of the period, flying the three-seat DH80A Puss Moth G-ABJU, a type which gained fame in

the hands of the record breakers Amy Johnson and Jim Mollison. Colonel Sempill could have had a very direct connection with Aldergrove during World War One, but for a change of plan. Handley Page O/400s were being built by the Standard Aircraft Corporation of Elizabeth, New Jersey in 1918, the first example being test flown by the Colonel. A bold and innovative plan had been hatched to fly the completed aircraft across the Atlantic to Aldergrove, but with the ending of the war the idea was shelved.

In an interview which appeared in the *Belfast Telegraph*, in July 1933, Sir Alan commented that the site at Sydenham was as yet unsuitable for sustained commercial use and needed much more work. He went on: "Every part of the Empire has got its air ports. It seems to me that if we can have an air route to Australia and an air route right through to South Africa, then something is wrong when this marvellous part of the Empire, Ulster, cannot have a regular air route to London."[29] Between 1932 and 1937 Sir Alan Cobham and his aircraft travelled the British Isles and gave more than 1,200 public displays, being seen by over four million spectators and carrying almost one million passengers on pleasure flights, in pursuit of his aim "to popularise flying with the public and indeed, to make everybody interested in flying".[30]

Civil Aviation Again

An unsung hero of this period was the Scotsman John C Sword. He established Midland and Scottish Air Ferries (M&S) in 1933, using DH83s G-ACBZ/CB/CT/CU initially. On 28 March and 27 April 'route-proving' flights were flown by John Rae from Glasgow to Dublin (Baldonnel) by way of Aldergrove in G-ACBZ. The first service was from Glasgow to Campbeltown on 18 April, to which route Belfast was soon added and on 31 May the first regular civil air service arrived at Aldergrove. The flights operated twice daily in the summer months, leaving Renfrew at 9.00 am and 6.00 pm, making the return journey at 10.30 am and 7.30 pm. Hired Rolls Royce or Daimler limousines provided free transport to the respective city centres. To begin with the fares were £3.00 single and £5.00 return. A reduction to £3 10s 0d (£3.50) return was made in December 1933. Children were charged half fare. The trial flight for the press was made on Tuesday 30 May and was reported on in highly favourable terms by the representatives of both the *Belfast Telegraph* and the *Belfast Newsletter*. The aircraft on the outward leg to Glasgow was the Avro 618/Ten G-ACGF, a licence-built version of the Fokker FVII. It was described by the *Telegraph* reporter thus:

> The company have a fleet of twelve commercial aircraft, the largest of which is the Avro Ten, a beautiful machine and the last word in luxury. It is a ten-seater, fitted with three Armstrong Siddeley Lynx engines, developing a total of nearly 700 hp. It has a wingspan of over 70 feet. An important feature of the aircraft is that if for any reason one of its engines should fail, the machine will continue as [if] nothing had happened, equipped as it is with special navigational instruments which enable the pilot to fly through any weather and in any circumstances.[31]

The writer may be guilty here of a little exaggeration and was equally taken by the interior fit: "Other accessories include a very efficient Marconi wireless installation. The passenger cabin is attractively decorated in silver and red

M & S advert.   *J Woods Collection*

and each passenger has a seat beside a window enabling him to have a magnificent view of the sea and the country. Above each seat is a ventilator for individual use and there are light luggage racks as well as accommodation for heavier baggage."[32]

The *Newsletter* takes up the story of the flight: "Punctually at noon, the pilot, Mr. J. H. Orrell, opened his throttles and the big aeroplane ran smoothly into the wind, gathering speed until its curved wings bore us aloft in flight.

Avro 618/Ten of Midland and Scottish.   *AJ Jackson*

The stricken de Havilland DH84 in a "field near Antrim" on 14 September 1933.   *AJ Jackson*

The machine climbed steadily and the aerodrome buildings seemed to slide away. The pilot operated a winch which let out a weighted wireless aerial and telegraphic communication was instantly established with all air stations."[33] On arrival in Glasgow after a flight of one hour and ten minutes, the party proceeded to Glasgow for lunch and were then treated to a coach tour. The return flight that evening in the DH Dragon G-ACCZ, piloted by Edward Stewart, was described by the *Newsletter* as "if anything more enjoyable...we crossed the Ulster coast at Cushendall and a splendid view of the Glens of Antrim was presented. In a minute one is able to see more of the beauties of Ulster from the air than in a week by any other means."[34] The *Telegraph*'s man agreed: "I will never forget this, my first flight and I will certainly look forward to further opportunities for seeing the country from the higher

altitudes."[35]

The pilot of that first flight, JH 'Jimmy' Orrell, had a remarkable flying career, beginning in 1926, flying Sopwith Snipes as a sergeant pilot in the RAF. He then became a 'barnstormer' before starting his airline career with M&S, which continued with Imperial Airways' European and Empire routes and the legendary wartime ball-bearing runs to Sweden for BOAC. He then became a test pilot for Avro, making the initial flights on over 900 Lancasters and moving on to the Shackleton, Tudor and Vulcan.

M&S advertised the service as 'The Irish Scot', with the following sales pitch: "...it allows salesmen and others to leave Glasgow at 9.00 a.m., have over seven hours in Belfast or ten hours in Kintyre and be back in Glasgow by 9.15 p.m.".[36] Day returns from Campbeltown to Belfast were priced at £2 10s 0d (£2.50).

By September, three Dragons – G-ACCZ, G-ACDL and G-ACDN – were the main aircraft on the route, with one of these overnighting at Aldergrove. An unfortunate accident happened on 14 September, when 'CCZ, flown by Ed Stewart, suffered an engine failure soon after take-off and made a forced landing in a field near Antrim. The aircraft was badly damaged, but luckily there were no serious injuries.

A winter schedule was maintained and in a press interview John Sword spoke of the importance of radio communications in improving air safety, and called for the establishment of a radio station at Renfrew. "In the meantime", he stated, "we have equipped ourselves with a powerful searchlight which we use for night landings. An aeroplane is able to leave Aldergrove Aerodrome, near Belfast, at nine o'clock at night and within ten miles of the

De Havilland DH84.   *Flight*

Airspeed Ferry.   *AJ Jackson*

Ayrshire coast, the pilot has been able to pick out Renfrew by the beam of the searchlight."[37]

In December 1933, when Renfrew was temporarily closed by fog and snow for a fortnight, M&S used the landing field at Monkton – a location which now lies under the main runway of Prestwick International Airport. The field was picked by a great friend of Sword's, Jimmy Jeffs, whose name will appear again in this story.

The next major development for Aldergrove was on 27 March 1934, with the establishment of a Liverpool–Isle of Man–Belfast service which would use not only the Dragon and Avro Ten aircraft but also the Airspeed Ferrys G-ACBT and G-ACFB. The Ferrys' regular pilot was Nigel Pelly, whose family hailed from Co Londonderry and who had learned to fly with 502 Squadron at Aldergrove in 1927. He was apparently a very keen pipe smoker, even while flying, and his cockpit could be readily identified by the presence of burnt matches in the map pockets. The Ferry had been the first aircraft purchased by M&S – it was powered by three engines and could carry nine passengers. Only four of this type were built, as the Dragon proved to be a much more capable and economic design. A point of interest is that the joint managing director of Airspeed was NS Norway, who later found fame as the novelist Neville Shute.

The End of a Brave Venture

Sadly, the advent of Railway Air Services (RAS), which was owned by the four main railway companies and Imperial Airways, marked the end of the line for John Sword, who was 'encouraged' to return to his original business of motor transport. This was at a time when he was starting a route between Glasgow, Belfast, the Isle of Man, Liverpool and London (though to be more precise, the service was from Romford in Essex), which had commenced on 9 April 1934. This development had been

celebrated in some style a few days earlier by the Prime Minister, Ramsay MacDonald, who had flown from Castle Bromwich to Liverpool in the Midland and Scottish Avro 642 G-ACFV to attend an inaugural dinner with the Air Minister and civic dignitaries from Glasgow, Belfast, Liverpool, Birmingham and the Isle of Man.

The plans laid by John Sword and Edward Hillman were truly revolutionary for their day, with Speke Airport, Liverpool acting as a 'hub' and connecting services by Hillman's Airways from Romford to Le Bourget, Paris and by the Dutch airline KLM from Liverpool to Amsterdam.

Occasionally the pride of the M&S fleet, the sleek and beautiful 16-passenger Avro 642, named *The Marchioness of Londonderry*, undertook the Aldergrove run. One of the M&S engineers, JR Hesketh, recalled:

> Another memorable flight was from Romford in G-ACFV on 12th April 1934 to Hooton and then on to Aldergrove. Capt. Malet was the pilot and I was the flight engineer. The passengers were Lord and Lady Londonderry, the weather report for Aldergrove was bad – base of cloud 300 ft. with poor visibility, but as his Lordship had a very important conference in Belfast that evening we pressed on and proceeded on a time factor for let down having flown above cloud across the Irish Sea. We started to descend, hoping to break cloud and having reached 1000 ft. with no sign of a break, we turned 90 degrees to starboard to position us out to sea NE of Belfast. His Lordship sensed that we had altered course, came up into the cockpit and suggested that we could land on his own strip at Mount Stewart if Aldergrove was impossible. We got down under the low cloud and proceeded up Belfast Lough to Carrickfergus and then round the back of Divis at approx. 200 ft. to Aldergrove. There was quite a reception party to greet them and when he got out, Lord Londonderry told them what a good flight they had had. Malet and I later mused over the thought of landing the 642 on the short grass strip at Mount Stewart.[38]

On another occasion, on 19 May 1934, the 642 made the journey from Renfrew in only 50 minutes. The only pilot allowed to fly the big Avro was Squadron Leader HGR Malet DFC, a distinguished pilot but of such short stature that he had to stand up while taxying the aircraft in order to see where he was going.

The final M&S schedules to Aldergrove were flown by Nigel Pelly from Speke and Renfrew respectively on 10 and 11 July 1934.

Avro 642 *Marchioness of Londonderry.*   *H Holmes Collection*

The Midland and Scottish GPO mail contract for the London (now based at the 'Essex Air Port' Stapleford), Liverpool and Belfast route was taken over by Hillman's Airways on 16 July 1934. Several of the M&S pilots were taken on by Edward Hillman. Soon it was running in parallel with a RAS service.

Railway Air Services

The first RAS schedule – between Croydon (London), Castle Bromwich (Birmingham), Barton (Manchester), Aldergrove and Renfrew (Glasgow) – was flown by the DH86s G-ACVY *Mercury* and G-ACPL *Diana* on 20 August 1934. In control of the Aldergrove operation was Mr AB Wood, the Inspector in Charge. The aircraft were met by the Lord Mayor, Sir Crawford McCullagh, to whom Sir Harold Hartley, vice-president of the LMS Railway Co, handed the first bag of mail. Under the command of Captain JH Lock *Mercury* left Aldergrove shortly before 11.00 am, the first fare-paying passenger being Mr TE White of Dungiven. *Diana* was flown by Captain E Poole. This aircraft, which was the prototype, had been chartered by RAS from Imperial Airways, as the second DH86 ordered for RAS, G-ACVZ *Jupiter*, had not yet been delivered. The *Imperial Airways Staff News* of 22 August 1934 commented as follows:

Avro 642 seating arrangement.   *H Holmes Collection*

The volume of mail and the number of passengers on the first service made it necessary to operate the service from Glasgow to Croydon in duplicate and despite the fact that a violent storm of rain and wind was being experienced at Glasgow at the advertised time of departure, the two air-liners left to schedule. Although most adverse weather conditions were encountered they completed their flight to Belfast and left again for Manchester. Over the Irish Sea they ran into the centre of the depression and weather conditions became abnormal. The wind reached gale force and dislocated steamship services, and when the air-liners arrived at Manchester after a stormy flight, it was decided that the conditions made it

De Havilland DH86 *Mercury* of Railway Air Services.

Mercury's sister de Havilland DH86, *Jupiter*. *AJ Jackson*

inadvisable to proceed to Birmingham and Croydon. The mails were therefore sent on by train. The gale abated during the evening and enabled the aircraft to proceed from Manchester to their scheduled positions in order to carry out the following day's services.[39]

Sir Harold Hartley himself could have testified to the severity of the weather conditions, as at one stage the aircraft hit turbulence which caused it to descend several hundred feet with such rapidity that he was thrown against the cabin roof. His head struck the muslin covered escape hatch through which he partially and briefly emerged into the airstream. After this somewhat tempestuous start, the service went from strength to strength and after the initial proving period its operation was extended until further notice. RAS also maintained a mail and freight-only connecting service between Belfast, the Isle of Man and

Manchester during August and September, using the DH84 Dragon II G-ACXI.

On 30 August 1934, a distinguished visitor, Mr Ramsay MacDonald, arrived at Aldergrove and was received by Wing Commander LTN Gould MC, the Officer Commanding 502 Squadron. His destination was Mount Stewart, to which he was conveyed by air in a DH Puss Moth of Airwork Ltd.

Following a series of crashes involving DH86s in Australia, the type was withdrawn from service in the middle of November for a precautionary inspection. While this was in progress, the Westland Wessex G-AAGW was chartered from Imperial Airways and used on the Belfast service for about ten days. The Wessex was a boxy, high-wing, three-engine monoplane and was much slower than the DH86, with a smaller passenger capacity. From November, the DH86s terminated their part of the route in Belfast and the connection to Glasgow was flown using DH84s. Liverpool was substituted for Manchester in the route structure. *Jupiter* replaced *Diana* in December 1934. All three DH86s were the short-nosed, single-pilot version, with a radio operator's position to the rear of the cockpit. *Diana* was converted to twin-pilot configuration, renamed *Delphinus* and subsequently served with Imperial Airways.

The Ards Airport

The 'Ards Airport', a new, purpose built civil aerodrome, was officially opened on 31 August 1934 at Newtownards in Co Down. Its establishment owed much to Lord Londonderry, who made part of his estate available and was closely involved in the plans for the airport. The opening ceremony featured 502 Squadron, with three Vickers Virginias contributing to a small flying display. Services were gradually transferred there from Aldergrove, beginning with the Hillman's operation, and thus ended the first phase of its life as a civil airport on 23 May 1936, when RAS moved to Ards. Before the transfer DH89 Rapides had been introduced as back-up aircraft to the DH86s. Interestingly, before the demise of Midland and Scottish, John Sword had conducted negotiations with the Belfast Corporation regarding the feasibility of using the Malone site again, as he was aware that the Air Ministry were keen for Aldergrove to revert to purely military use. These negotiations came to nothing, firstly because Malone's drainage problems would have required considerable expenditure to solve; while secondly, John Sword was spending a considerable amount of money already on his, perhaps, over-ambitious airline; and thirdly, the authorities favoured RAS and Newtownards.

The Ards airport, Newtownards, Co Down, with the famous landmark Scrabo Tower in the background.   *T Maddock Collection*

Services to Ards were provided by Hillman's Airways and United Airways, which were merged into British Airways in 1936. This resulted in their connections to Glasgow, Blackpool, the Isle and Man and Liverpool being passed over to George Nicholson's Northern and Scottish Airways, which was affiliated to the same group, all controlled by Whitehall Securities. In a further reorganisation, in May 1937, these routes again changed hands, passing to Railway Air Services and its associate company, the Manx Airway. All civil flights were now concentrated at Ards. For a time, competition to Blackpool and the Isle of Man was offered by Blackpool and West Coast Air Services, but during 1937 Isle of Man Air Services (IoMAS) took control and also assimilated the Manx Airway. This put all business in the hands of RAS and IoMAS, which was a 'Railway Associated Airline'.

The most commonly used civil aircraft of the period were the twin-engine DH84 Dragon, the four-engine DH86 Express Airliner and the DH89 Dragon Rapide, which was a development of the DH84. These types were the catalysts which ignited the advance of British civil aviation in the 1930s, and had a number of attractive features: they were reliable; they could carry an economically viable load of passengers and cargo; they were relatively inexpensive to purchase and maintain; and they could operate from small, rough fields as well as civil aerodromes. The first Dragon flew in 1932, while the final Rapide retired from airline service with British European Airways in 1964. Honourable mention should also be made of the Spartan Cruisers, three-engine six–eight passenger monoplanes, which gave sterling service throughout the UK from 1933 until the war began.

Air Days and New Aircraft

From 1934 until just before the war broke out Aldergrove was opened to the public every year for 'Empire Air Day' in late May. These were very popular events, with many thousands attending. Special buses were operated from Belfast to the airfield and the entrance fee was a modest one shilling (5p). A participant at the 'Air Day' in 1935 was the famous Scottish pilot Captain David Barclay, who made his first landing at Aldergrove in a DH84 G-ACFG of Northern and Scottish Airways. Barclay's logbook entry noted a transit time from Glasgow of one hour and ten minutes and then a total of an hour and 45 minutes joy-riding. David Barclay became one of the pioneers of the Air Ambulance service in the

Highlands and Islands of Scotland. For over 30 years he flew missions of mercy in all weather conditions and thereby saved many lives. With each new show the event became progressively more elaborate, with greater participation from RAF units on the mainland. Visiting types of aircraft which were new to the Ulster public included the Vickers Vildebeeste, Hawker Demon, Vickers Wellington and, in 1939, the Supermarine Spitfire.

Before they retired, the Virginias took part in a further

Westland Wallaces of 502 Squadron flying over the Royal Ulster Yacht Club in Bangor, Co Down.   *J Hewitt Collection*

Handley Page Heyford and aircrew.   *E Cromie Collection*

502 Squadron crew en route to their aircraft.   *RG Spencer*

Royal ceremony, when the Duke of Gloucester, who was also the Earl of Ulster, paid a three-day visit to Northern Ireland in May 1935, representing the King and Queen as part of the Silver Jubilee celebrations. Three aircraft escorted HMS *Achilles*, as the cruiser brought the Duke up Belfast Lough.

From October 1935 502 Squadron was able to demonstrate a changed role, and a more modern type of aircraft, when it became a single-engine bomber squadron. The Westland Wallace, 11 of which were on strength, had gained fame two years before, when two specially adapted versions had become the first aircraft to fly over the 29,028 ft peak of Mount Everest. It had a crew of two and could carry up to 1,000 lbs of bombs.

On 28 January 1936, Aldergrove officially became a Royal Air Force Station, under the command of Group Captain JC Russell DSO.

For a few months in the same year, 502 was joined by 9 Squadron from Andover in Hampshire, while it was changing its aircraft from Vickers Virginias to Handley Page Heyfords. It was joined by 102, another Heyford squadron, for a few months at the end of the year. The Heyford was a remarkable looking aircraft, a large twin-engine biplane heavy bomber, but with the fuselage attached to the upper rather than the lower wing, massive 'spats' lessening some of the aerodynamic drag of the fixed undercarriage and a retractable 'dustbin' turret extending down from the rear fuselage.

A Gloster Gauntlet of the 'Met Flight'.   *E Cromie Collection*

The Met Flight and Changes for 502

Another development in 1936 was the establishment of a Meteorological Flight. This was the second such unit to be formed, with the first being at Duxford in Cambridgeshire. The unit was equipped with Bristol Bulldogs, which had first been introduced into service in 1929. Considering that the job was to go aloft in all weathers to 20,000 ft, the pilots were a hardy and special breed. The first officer in command of the Met Flight was of that stamp, Flight Lieutenant Victor Beamish of

Hawker Hinds on patrol.   *E Cromie Collection*

Coleraine. The aim of the Met Flight was not only to find out what the forecast was, but also to help with the study of weather systems which built up in the Atlantic and so develop a greater understanding of the patterns of depression and anticyclone which dominate our lives and conversation. Flying Officer Denys Gillam, who was the deputy flight leader, described the work as follows:

> For a year and a half we never missed a flight to 20,000 feet every day, regardless of the weather. Apart from the difficulty of getting reliable bearings on the wireless, blind flying presented difficulties as we had no gyro instruments, only a turn and bank indicator, air speed indicator and altitude meter. We had a wet and a dry bulb for air temperatures, attached to a strut on our machines and we watched these and wrote the readings every 1000 feet. We would also report on cloud levels. We were really looking for inversions of temperatures. I suppose it was my happiest time in the Air Force.[40]

As the result of several crashes (one of which involved Denys Gillam in a blizzard among the Mourne Mountains, and from which he was lucky to walk away) the Bulldogs were replaced in July 1937 with the more powerful Gloster Gauntlet, a type which has the distinction of being the last of the RAF's long line of open-cockpit, biplane fighters. They had more powerful engines, climbed much faster than the Bulldogs and coped considerably better with the demanding and specialised task.

Victor Beamish was awarded the Air Force Cross for his work in forming the flight and later returned to mainstream duties. He commanded the fighter station of North Weald during 1940, where one of his squadron commanders was the legendary Bob Stanford Tuck, who said of Beamish: "I tried to emulate Victor, because I considered him one of the

best commanders I'd known. He was the kind of man you came to trust completely, the kind of man you tried to be like in every possible way."[40] Sadly, Victor Beamish did not survive the war, but died in action, a Group Captain with the Distinguished Service Order and bar, as well as the Distinguished Flying Cross.

In 1937 502 squadron was re-equipped again, this time with the Hawker Hind, which was a development of their famous and aesthetically pleasing Hart. It was still, however, a biplane, with open cockpits for its crew of two, made of fabric-covered steel and aluminium and having a top speed of 186 mph. Two Avro Tutors and a Hart were also received for use by the squadron training flight. A change in status from being Special Reserve to becoming an Auxiliary Air Force Squadron occurred on 1 July. The following year, the Marquis of Londonderry was appointed Honorary Air Commodore. Also in 1938, on 16 March, the squadron participated in the official opening of the new civil airport for the province (replacing Newtownards) – Belfast Harbour at Sydenham. Five Hawker Hinds joined six Bristol Blenheims of 139 Squadron and six Fairey Battles of 52 Squadron in providing the flying display. The scheduled flights from there were flown by Railway Air Services to Glasgow, Liverpool, Manchester, Birmingham, Stoke-on-Trent (on request) and London, with Isle of Man Air Services connecting the Isle of Man and Blackpool.

Tom Grant, aged 18, joined 502 Squadron in 1938 and trained as an air gunner. He began flying in the Hind and remembers practising over the Lough Neagh ranges, as well as training sorties over Portrush, the north-west and the Ards Peninsula. A design peculiarity of the Hind was the bomb aimer's position, which was below the pilot's seat. He had to crawl underneath, while the pilot operated a hand crank to raise the radiator, which otherwise obscured the downward view. The bomb aimer then had to be not only

Westland Wallace.   *E Cromie Collection*

502 Squadron pilots preparing for flight.

J Hewitt Collection

accurate but also swift, as unless the radiator was lowered again speedily, the engine would overheat. Tom has fond memories of the Hind, which he recalls as a delightfully aerobatic aircraft.

The Re-supply of Rathlin

The Met Flight also distinguished itself in 1938, when torrential rain and persistent gale force winds resulted in the inhabitants of Rathlin Island being cut off for three weeks from re-supply by boat from Ballycastle. The islanders radioed for help. A Met Flight Gauntlet K5283, flown by Denys Gillam, responded to the government's plea for assistance. He flew a reconnaissance of the most likely landing field, which was only 250 yards long. While he was in the air SD Bell and Company of Ann Street, Belfast, had

SD Bell's opportune advert at the time of the Rathlin airlift.

Westland Wallace target-towing over Lough Neagh.

E Cromie Collection

Hawker Henley 3BGS. *R Burrows Collection*

Fairy Swordfish of 774 NAS on gunnery exercise.

R Burrows Collection

Blackburn Roc of 774 NAS. *I Henderson Collection*

prepared a consignment of flour, oatmeal, butter, tea, sugar, lard, paraffin oil, candles, matches, cigarettes and newspapers, which was conveyed by express van to Aldergrove. This was then loaded into the Westland Wallace K5073 and Denys Gillam took off again. In the meantime, a message had been wired to the local priests: "An attempt will be made to land food from an aeroplane at about 2.30 pm this afternoon. Please light a fire to make smoke for the guidance of the aeroplane."[42] The *Belfast Telegraph* described the first landing by an aircraft on Rathlin as follows: "To make the landing the plane had to descend very low and hurdle over the roof of a house. The field selected for landing was the best available but it was small and exceptionally bumpy and definitely hazardous for a medium sized bomber."[43]

The feat was repeated the next day in another Wallace K5074. Denys Gillam was later awarded the Air Force Cross for his work with the Met Flight and for his airmanship and bravery in undertaking the relief flights. Subsequently he served with great distinction throughout the war, becoming a Group Captain and adding a DSO and two bars, as well as the DFC and bar to his medal tally. SD Bell did not miss their opportunity either, as an advert appeared in the newspapers headed "Rathlin Island – supplied at a moment's notice – we can supply your requirements with the same dispatch and satisfaction."[44]

War Clouds

In March 1936, as part of its expansion programme due to the increasing likelihood of another European war, the RAF set up an Armament Training Camp at Aldergrove. Fairly rudimentary target facilities already existed on the eastern shore of Lough Neagh to meet the needs of 502 Squadron. These were developed and expanded to provide for practice and live bombing, as well as air to air and air to ground firing. The initial establishment of No 2 Armament

Training camp was Westland Wallaces. Later aircraft on the strength of the unit, which became No 2 Armament Training School (2 ATS) in 1938, included Fairey Battles and Hawker Henleys. Up to the end of 1939, for periods of two or three weeks at a time, at least 35 different units of the Royal Air Force and Fleet Air Arm visited Aldergrove. The types of aircraft involved included Avro Ansons; Bristol Bulldogs and Blenheims; Handley Page Harrows and Heyfords; Fairey Hendons, Gordons and Swordfish; Hawker Demons, Furys, Hinds, Hectors and Hurricanes; Gloster Gauntlets and Gladiators; Blackburn Rocs, Sharks, and Skuas; Armstrong Whitworth Whitleys; and Westland Wallaces. In April, No 1 ATS and No 2 ATS combined to become No 3 Air Observers School, which in turn was reconstituted as No 3 Bombing and Gunnery School in November 1939. This heralded the return of a few Handley Page Heyfords as operational training aircraft until the school was disbanded in May 1940. Six of these were then put to a useful but rather ignominious purpose, when their wings were chopped off and the aircraft fuselages positioned as guardposts for perimeter defence. The school was also joined by 774 Naval Air Squadron on Christmas Day 1939, with Fairy Swordfish, Blackburn Roc, Shark and Skua aircraft to provide Telegraphist Air Gunner training. It has the distinction of being the first Fleet Air Arm squadron to be based in Northern Ireland.

No 23 MU

Before an aircraft was ready for military use it had to pass from the manufacturers through a service Maintenance Unit (MU). In November 1939 No 23 MU was established at Aldergrove. The job of the MUs, which were largely civilian staffed, was to ready aircraft for operational or second line duties, fit armament and radios or carry out other specific modifications. Aircraft also needed regular maintenance that neither squadron nor station engineering staff could provide. They were then stored to await delivery to their unit. The first aircraft to receive the attention of 23 MU was a Bristol Bombay, one of 50 of this bomber/transport built under contract by Short and Harland. Thereafter expansion was rapid and within the first year the ten hangars occupied by the MU had received over 500 aircraft, of which more than 300 had been passed on to service duties.

Bristol Bombays under construction at the Short Brothers factory in Belfast.

Shorts

Chapter 3

Aldergrove at War

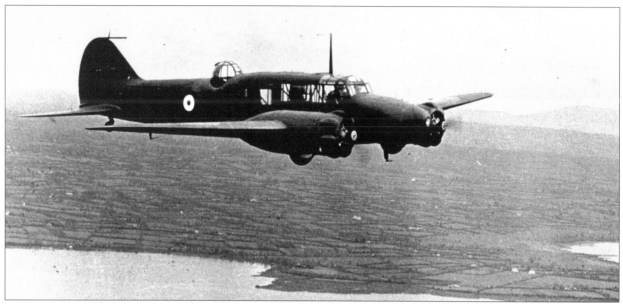

Avro Anson N5104 pictured over Co Antrim.

RG Spencer

502 Squadron Prepares for Active Duty

With the prospect of war looming ever closer, 502 Squadron received a monoplane aircraft for the first time, in January 1939. Over the next eight months 19 Avro Ansons were delivered. They took part in the last Empire Air Day in May of that year. The function of the squadron was also changed to reconnaissance and it became part of 18 Group Coastal Command in November 1938 and then 15 Group in June 1939. The Group was headquartered at Plymouth and consisted of two Anson and three Sunderland squadrons, responsible for patrolling St George's Channel, the Irish Sea and the North Atlantic coast of Ireland, searching for U-boats and protecting convoys. The first U-boat sighting was made in the early days of the war, on 24 September, close to Rathlin Island by OC B Flight, Flt Lieut Philip Billing, in Anson N5104. It was attacked as it submerged but no hits were observed.

The Avro Anson served with the Royal Air Force for over 30 years in a great variety of tasks. In the early months of

the war it proved very useful in the coastal patrol role before concentrating on its greater function as a training aircraft for wireless operators, air gunners and navigators. Tom Grant had also progressed to the Anson and completed patrols of up to seven hours duration. An unusual item which formed part of the aircraft's equipment was a carrier pigeon. This was intended to be released in the event of a ditching at sea – it would then (hopefully) fly home and alert the air-sea rescue service. The birds had to be trained for this task and were taken aloft for 'air experience'. It became apparent that even the modest cruising speed of the Anson was too fast to launch the pigeon successfully from an aperture in the floor by the bomb aimer's position. They suffered severe injuries in the slipstream. A solution was found by wrapping the bird in layers of toilet paper – by the time it had unravelled, the pigeon was clear of the onrush of air and could proceed safely on its journey to base. Tom subsequently flew two tours of operations with Bomber Command in Whitleys and Wellingtons and his name will figure again in the Aldergrove story.

The Ansons of 502 Squadron were backed up by the DH Tiger Moths of 4 Coastal Patrol Flight which, though unarmed, slow and vulnerable, carried out inshore spotting duties for a few months, though they chiefly operated from Hooton Park, Liverpool, along with a detachment of Ansons.

Cheshire VC

In September 1940 a detachment of Whitleys from 102 Squadron arrived. Among the young pilots was Leonard Cheshire. The future commanding officer of 617 Squadron, winner of the Victoria Cross and founder of the Cheshire Homes, was not impressed by anti-submarine patrols. His biographer, Andrew Boyle, graphically describes the routine: "Crews had to stand by permanently ready to take off at any hour of the day or night. The plodding, eye-straining monotony of Atlantic patrols and convoy escorts five hundred feet above the heaving swell and the tossing lines of merchant ships was a grim, thankless duty that drained the mind and frayed the nerves."[43]

On 5 October Cheshire experienced something of a break in the monotony. His aircraft was dispatched in a hurry from Aldergrove in the teeth of a storm to locate a missing convoy. He only had two other crew members, the wireless operator and the navigator, rather than the usual four. They had no parachutes and a single flying helmet between them. Having found the convoy in atrocious weather, they spent the next few hours flying around it at mast height (having nearly collided with a destroyer, it had seemed prudent to fly a little higher than wave top level which Cheshire had first selected). Navigation home was

principally by guesswork and fuel was running low. A radio message at last came through: "It's O.K. You're over land now. Jump."[46] With the lack of parachutes onboard, this was a rather unhelpful instruction. By an enormous stroke of luck a small gap in the clouds appeared, they glimpsed the Aldergrove flarepath lights and landed safely after a 12½ hour flight. The squadron hierarchy were undecided as to whether Cheshire should be awarded a rocket or a medal. Soon afterwards, 102 Squadron returned to England.

War Work

In late 1940 the Ansons were replaced by one of the RAF's least heralded types, the Blackburn Botha, a three-seat, twin-engine reconnaissance bomber, which proved to be more of a danger to its crews than the Germans. Thankfully, after only a few months, the squadron began to receive Armstrong Whitworth Whitley Mk Vs. These were powered by a pair of Rolls Royce Merlin engines, had a crew of five, a top speed of 222 mph and a range of 1,650 miles, with a bomb load of 3,000 lbs. Instead of having to rely on the flashing morse code of an Aldis lamp to communicate with convoy vessels, they had short range radio, but the biggest advance was the provision of ASV (Air to Surface Vessel) radar. These aircraft of 502 Squadron were the first Whitleys to be fitted with radar, in early 1941. Success soon came when, in February, U-93 was seriously damaged by a squadron aircraft after the initial acquisition of the target was made by radar, but by this time 502 had left Aldergrove and was operating from the newly constructed airfield at Limavady.

Armstrong Whitworth Whitley P5062.   *E Cromie Collection*

RAF Aldergrove in 1940.   *E Cromie Collection*

Hawker Hurricanes of 245 Squadron.   *I Henderson Collection*

Fighter Station

With the overall war position looking somewhat gloomy early in 1940, and with the RAF's resources considerably overstretched, no fighter aircraft could be spared for the protection of the province. To cover the gap, the Bombing and Gunnery School was reorganised into a fighter squadron with Blackburn Rocs and Skuas; two medium bomber squadrons with Fairey Battles; and a reconnaissance squadron with Fairey Swordfish and Blackburn Sharks.

In July 1940 Fighter Command allocated 245 Squadron the task of providing for the air defence of Belfast, as well as convoy protection duties. They were equipped with the famous Hawker Hurricane which, together with the Supermarine Spitfire, will always be remembered for its role in the Battle of Britain. The Hurricane Mk I was armed with eight Browning machine guns and its 979 hp Rolls Royce Merlin engine gave it a top speed of over 300 mph. The first few months were given over to training new pilots and bringing the squadron to a state of operational readiness. A temporary Fighter Sector HQ was also set up

at Aldergrove. Towards the end of the year the squadron received a new commanding officer, Squadron Leader John Simpson DFC, who had previously been very active with 43 Squadron (coincidentally the same as Sholto Douglas, Aldergrove's 'founder', 23 years before). S/L Simpson had

245 Squadron CO's aircraft, *Joker.*   *I Henderson Collection*

scored ten 'kills' and his experience helped to give the squadron an edge that was soon needed in the tragic events that were to unfold in April 1941. The squadron first sighted an enemy aircraft on 4 February, near Rathlin Island. It was a Heinkel 111, but flying at 30,000 feet it was too high to intercept.

On the night of 7–8 April came the first of the five raids of the 'Belfast Blitz', which caused such death and destruction to the city. Although not equipped for night-fighting, 245 Squadron took to the air. To avoid collisions all sorties were flown by single aircraft, which was why S/L Simpson was on his own, in his personal Hurricane with its insignia, a joker holding the Ace of Spades, when he sighted two aircraft above him at 7,000 ft. His own words graphically convey the experience:

> I could see them because as they moved, they obliterated the stars. Whether enemy or not I was unable to tell. So I flew nearer and learned soon enough. The rear gunners of both aircraft fired on me at the same time. There was a shower of bullets, some tracer, some glowing red. It was my first experience of being fired on in the dark and I didn't like it. I took avoiding action and crept down to attack the rearmost of them. Then came my next surprise. I had never fired my guns in the dark before. There was a god-awful flash, quite blinding. In daylight one does not see it. At night it is terrific and I was so blinded that I lost sight of my Hun.[47]

When Simpson recovered his night vision, he re-sighted the enemy:

> It was in a perfect position for me so I opened fire once more. This time I prepared for the flash of my guns and kept my eyes on him. His rear gunner opened fire but only for a second as I apparently got him. Then I saw a comforting glow in the belly of the aircraft. Below the glow was hanging an immense object. I could see the silhouette of it. I suppose it must have been a heavy bomb or mine and I think I must have hit it for the Heinkel blew up with a terrific explosion. I found out afterwards that bits of metal from the Hun had hit my left wing and had made a tear in the fuselage by the tailplane.[48]

S/L Simpson shot down a Junkers 88 near Ardglass on the 5–6 May and in recognition of his two night victories, and his leadership of the squadron, he was awarded a bar to his DFC on 10 May. Score number 13 followed on 13 May – a Dornier 17 over the sea off Larne. Fatigued by his

extensive combat duties, S/L Simpson was rested in June and posted to a group staff job. He ended the war as a Group Captain, but tragically took his own life not long afterwards, a victim of the stress endured by so many.

According to a report which appeared in the national press in February 1999, two 245 Squadron pilots were involved in one of the great mysteries of the war, the flight of Rudolf Hess, Hitler's deputy, from Germany to Scotland in 1941. In the early evening of 10 May, Sgts Vaclav Bauman and Leopold Srom (two of the 87 Czech fighter pilots who flew for the RAF after escaping the German invasion of their country in 1939) were scrambled from Aldergrove to intercept an intruder over southern Scotland. As they closed in and identified the aircraft as a Messerschmitt Bf110, they were abruptly ordered to break off the attack and return to base. On landing, the two somewhat bemused Czechs asked S/L Simpson for an explanation. He, in turn, requested the same from Group HQ. A little later, an Anson landed at Aldergrove and the two sergeants were interrogated intensively. In the mess, speculation raged and was only satisfied by the arrival of a copy of the *Glasgow Daily Record*, which carried the headline, 'Rudolf Hess in Glasgow'. It appears that the official records were amended to remove all reference to this event, which has only come to light nearly 50 years later as a result of research in the Czech Republic, including access to the pilots' own logbooks.

In July 1941 245 Squadron was transferred to Ballyhalbert, where a fighter airfield and Sector HQ had been completed.

Donald Bennett

On 11 November 1940 a flight of seven Lockheed Hudsons landed at Aldergrove. With so many aircraft using the airfield's overworked facilities this would not have been remarkable, except that they had flown across the Atlantic from Newfoundland, on delivery from the manufacturers in California. This proved to be the start of the 'Transatlantic Ferry Service' between Britain and the USA, allowing the Allied forces to benefit more quickly and safely from the massive output of American factories. Previously, sea transport had been taking up to three months. Over the course of the war this first, regular, two-way (as the ferry crews were returned to the USA and Canada by Liberator) all year round route across the North Atlantic notched up some 2,000 crossings. The experience gained, of course, was vital in the post-war development of civil air transport across the oceans. Therefore, it can be claimed that

Aldergrove had a pivotal position at a defining moment of the conquest of the skies.

The leader of that first flight was Captain DCT Bennett, yet another name renowned in the history of aviation to be associated with Aldergrove. Before the war he had been a pilot with Imperial Airways and was involved in the early Atlantic crossings in the Short S23 C Class flying boats and the remarkable Short-Mayo Composite project, in which a fast seaplane, *Mercury*, was launched from the back of a flying boat, *Maia*. Bennett was the captain of *Mercury* on its non-stop flight from Foynes, in Co Clare, to Montreal on 21 July 1938. He commented on the Hudson delivery flight that "the whole navigation depended on me and I was aware of the fact that with practically no radio aids available, my sextant and myself were rather vital to the proceedings. The sense of heavy responsibility was somewhat peculiarly relieved by the knowledge that on this occasion, at least, one was appreciated."[49] In 1941 he joined the RAF and as a young Group Captain, in 1942, was appointed to create and lead the elite 'Pathfinder' Force which marked the targets in the heavy bomber offensive. However, back on that November day in 1940, the weary crews, after their nine and a half hour flight, were more interested in bacon and eggs in the mess and then being taken to the Grand Central Hotel in Belfast to rest before proceeding to Liverpool, Speke, the next day.

The Battle of the Atlantic

According to Sir Winston Churchill, writing in his war memoirs, this fighting ground was the battle on which the whole outcome of the war depended: "The only thing that ever frightened me during the war was the U-boat peril."[50] In this mighty struggle, Aldergrove played a full part. When France fell, in May 1940, the Germans had the great advantage that they could henceforth operate from bases much closer to the battleground and thus extend the radius of action, not only of their submarines but also of the long-range Focke Wulf Condor aircraft. Northern Ireland had a vital role to play as a forward base in the campaign, due to its geographical situation.

To begin with, detachments of several squadrons, including Bristol Blenheims of 254 Squadron, as well as

Bristol Beaufighter of 252 Squadron.   *RAF Aldergrove*

Lockheed Hudsons of 48 Squadron.   *RAF Aldergrove*

Lockheed Hudsons of 224 and 233 Squadrons, were based at Aldergrove for periods of up to several months. A new unit, 272 Squadron, formed at Aldergrove in November 1940, was equipped with Blenheims. Some material evidence of success was gained by the Hudsons of 233 Squadron, with the shooting down of a Heinkel 111 and a Condor in May and July 1941, both over the Atlantic. New and more potent aircraft arrived that year in the form of the Bristol Beaufighters of 143 and 252 Squadrons. This type was a long-range, twin-engine fighter, armed with four cannon and six machine guns.

Then 206 Squadron, with various marks of Hudson, stayed for ten months from August 1941 to June 1942. During that dark winter, before the tide of war began to turn, the squadron flew more than 100 sorties in a month on three occasions. Thirteen U-boats were sighted, eleven of which were attacked. However, in order to patrol the vast distances involved and to combat the U-boat 'wolf packs' far out into the Atlantic, it was recognised that four-engine, very long-range aircraft were necessary.

Vickers Wellingtons of 311 (Czech) Squadron.   *Imperial War Museum*

Bristol Beaufort.   *J Woods Collection*

Gloster Gladiator of the 'Met Flight'.   *J Woods Collection*

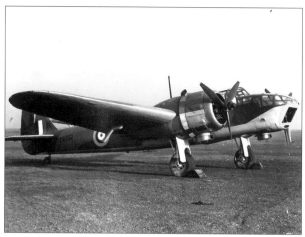

Bristol Blenheim.   *J Woods Collection*

A Mid-war Lull

Before Aldergrove could accommodate these larger, heavier types a major works programme had to be put in hand to replace the existing four runways with two new long paved runways, which in fact formed the basis of the layout that still exists. The work began in the autumn of 1941, but the airfield remained operational throughout the upheavals involved, though to a certain extent some of the burden had been lifted from Aldergrove with the opening of a large number of other airfields in the province since the start of the war. In 1939 there were only three aerodromes in the whole of Northern Ireland (Aldergrove, Belfast Harbour and Newtownards) – by 1941–42 they had been joined by a dozen more.

By July 1942 the Hudsons, Beaufighters and Blenheims had all departed. The Vickers Wellingtons of 311 (Czech) Squadron stayed briefly, but the main activity in this middle section of the war was concentrated on non-operational tasks – 23 MU was hard at work, and in July 1942 a record of 107 aircraft received attention; No 9 Operational Training Unit was formed to train Beaufighter and Beaufort crews before moving to England in September; and No 1 Armament Practice Camp had been formed to make use of the facilities on Lough Neagh.

In the meantime, the Met Flight carried on with its unobtrusive, unshowy, but vital work. The Gauntlets, which had given sterling, trouble-free service, had been replaced by Gloster Gladiators in December 1939. The Gladiator was perhaps the ultimate biplane fighter, certainly the last to serve with the RAF. It had an enclosed cockpit, a top speed of nearly 250 mph and four, rather than the conventional two, machine guns. By the start of

World War Two it was obsolete as a fighter, but performed heroically against the odds in Norway, the Western Desert, Greece and Malta. In January 1941 the Met unit was officially designated 1402 Flight and the following year its capabilities were enhanced by the provision of specially modified Supermarine Spitfires, which could climb to 38,000 ft. Interestingly, this was the only type of this famous aircraft which operated from Aldergrove during the war. There existed the requirement for much longer range aircraft, suitable for travelling far out into the Atlantic and obtaining scientifically measured data from the instruments and weather observers which they were large enough to carry. In March 1941 1405 Flight was formed at Aldergrove with Bristol Blenheims, which were not ideal for this role but were a useful stopgap. Other aircraft to serve with the Aldergrove Met Flights included Hudsons, Hurricanes and Handley Page Hampdens. Later, some of the rare Spitfire Mk VI and VII high altitude variants were supplied. These were capable of flying at 43,000 ft.

The Short Stirling

Following the Belfast Blitz in 1941, which caused damage to the Short and Harland flightsheds at Sydenham, some of the work was relocated to Aldergrove. Two hangars were set aside by 23 MU for the final assembly of Stirling bombers. The Inspector in Charge was Edward Body, who recalls recruiting many of his staff locally – including a blacksmith who became one of his best inspectors. A rate of five completed aircraft a month was achieved – these had to be test flown before being collected by the Air Transport Auxiliary for delivery to England.

Ted Body was delighted to become part of the flight

The famous Short Stirling bomber.

Shorts

team and so had the opportunity to fly several hundred hours in the right-hand seat of this famous aircraft – the first of Britain's wartime trio of four-engine heavy bombers – the Short Stirling, Handley Page Halifax and Avro Lancaster.

The company test pilots were Tom Brooke-Smith and George Wynne-Eaton. In their expert hands the lightly loaded Stirling was capable of considerable agility and could provide an impressive aerobatic spectacle. A Group Captain posted to Aldergrove for a rest from operations was treated to nearly vertical climbs, 'slides off the top', steep dives and 'third-flap circuits' within the airfield perimeter. On landing he expressed his appreciation of the "remarkable handling qualities" of the aeroplane. Ted Body also remembers the time when, over Lough Neagh, they were surprised to find a Met Flight Spitfire in formation just below the port wing. There then ensued 15 minutes of 'dogfighting' and hedgehopping, much to the entertainment of all concerned. On another occasion, the beloved flat cap habitually worn by George Wynne-Eaton blew out the window – they followed it down and pinpointed the field in which it had come to rest. Back at base, the pilot jumped into his car and made off at speed to recover his precious headgear.

Not all flights were fun. One day an electrical fault caused the undercarriage to malfunction – winding down the wheels with several hundred turns of a hand crank was no easy job. The Stirling gave good service to the RAF, but it could have been even better. It was always rather restricted as regards its service ceiling, partly due to Air Ministry insistence at the design stage that the wingspan should not exceed 100 ft rather than the planned 120 ft, so that it would fit into existing hangars.

A visiting US Liberator gave Ted Body a happy experience. As it was being towed into the hangar, the top sergeant asked, "Would any of you guys like an ice-cream?"[51] The aircraft was fitted with an on-board ice-cream maker!

The Shorts unit also had a Tiger Moth as a communications hack for trips to the main factory. Ted made good use of this, particularly as his future wife lived in Sydenham Avenue. The day he managed to remove several inches from both blades of the aircraft's propeller – firstly by hitting a pile of stones concealed in the grass and secondly, with a pocket knife to even it up – is not one of his prouder achievements. In all, some 1,213 Stirlings were manufactured in Belfast, of which several hundred took to the air for the first time from Aldergrove.

The U-boat Hunters

The first Very Long Range (VLR) aircraft to arrive at the newly enhanced Aldergrove were the Consolidated

Consolidated Liberator Mk IIIs of 120 Squadron.

RAF Aldergrove

A Boeing Fortress II of 220 Squadron.

Imperial War Museum

Liberator Mk IIIs of 120 Squadron and the Boeing B17 Flying Fortress IIs of 220 Squadron. Tangible success was achieved quickly, as by early March three U-boats had been sunk. Replacing 220 Squadron, 86 Squadron, also equipped with Liberators, added to the score with three more sinkings in April and May 1943. A third Liberator-equipped unit, 59 Squadron, made up the complement during this fine period in Aldergrove's history, with the destruction of six U-boats and several others badly damaged. Interestingly, the Liberator is perhaps less acclaimed than either the Flying Fortress or indeed the Avro Lancaster, but it served in every theatre of the war and was

constructed in greater numbers than either of its more famous contemporaries, with a total of 18,188 being built.

By the end of the year the Liberators had moved on and Aldergrove's main functions until the end of the war were concerned with training, maintenance and meteorology.

The Coming of Victory

In October 1943 No 1674 Heavy Conversion Unit (HCU) was formed. It moved to England soon afterwards, but came back to Aldergrove early in 1944, where it remained until the end of hostilities. Its task was to train crews in the operation of VLR types and the aircraft on strength included Handley Page Halifaxes, as well as Liberators and Fortresses.

A flavour of the aerial activity in and around Aldergrove towards the later stages of the war may be gained from examining the records of the Armament Practice Camp for a typical day – Saturday 22 April 1944. First on the scene in the morning were the Liberators of the HCU to drop 24 bombs; they were followed by Wellingtons from 407 Squadron at Limavady with another 36 bombs. In the afternoon the Liberators came back again with a further 47 bombs, to which could be added a Short Sunderland from 422 Squadron at Castle Archdale. While all of this multi-engine activity was going on, the Supermarine Seafire naval fighters from Long Kesh were busy unloading 89 bombs. But for inclement weather, which caused its cancellation, the late evening calm would have been shattered by a Leigh Light bombing exercise, carried out by more Liberators from 120 Squadron, Ballykelly. In all, there were 15 functionally different target zones dispersed throughout Lough Neagh.

Meanwhile the work of 23 MU continued, making its important contribution on hundreds of aircraft, including converting Short Stirling bombers to glider tugs and, from May 1944, working on the distinctive, gull-winged Chance Vought Corsair fighters for the Fleet Air Arm.

During the period 1939–45 Aldergrove served in a huge variety of roles, coping with many diverse types of work and aircraft. It is a record of which all concerned can be proud.

Sandeman's Ghost

In the last days of the war, airman Syd Frogley was posted to the Met Section at Aldergrove. His job was with the Upper Air Unit. Four times daily, hydrogen-filled balloons were released and tracked by radar to an altitude of 60,000 ft, monitoring the wind strength and direction at different levels, as well as making pressure, temperature and humidity measurements. Syd relates the following incident:

> I remember one 3 a.m. balloon ascent when a colleague and myself tried to start the diesel generator to power the radar. It was a clear moonlit night and as we were swinging the starting handle, we noticed a tall figure some 15 to 20 yards away.
>
> The engine proving reluctant to start, we called over for assistance, thinking it was the RAF security patrol but the still figure took no notice. Feeling a little peeved, I stopped what I was doing and walked over. As I got nearer, I saw that he was dressed in a dark cloak and a wide brimmed hat. I halted for a few moments, then as I moved forward again he just disappeared into the shadows.[52]

Both Syd and his colleague were puzzled, but they were not the last to see this apparition, which became familiarly known as Sandeman's Ghost, as he bore a resemblance to the famous figure on the eponymous port bottle. Having made some enquiries, they were later told by the local postmaster that there had been a coach hold up on that spot over 100 years before, at which there had been a brutal killing. The spectre they saw at the Upper Air Unit was thought to be the highwayman.

23 MU personnel pictured in front of a FAA Corsair.
RAF Aldergrove

Chapter 4

Post-War Days

Handley Page Halifax of 518 Squadron, Met Flight.

I Henderson Collection

Post-War Military Activity

On 18 September 1945, the Handley Page Halifaxes of 518 Squadron moved from the Scottish island of Tiree to Aldergrove. Their task was meteorological and as a larger unit the squadron absorbed the existing 1402 Flight, with Spitfire VIIs and Hurricane IICs, which had returned after a few months at Ballyhalbert. The Halifaxes were specially adapted for the very precise data collection required. They flew two 'Bismuth' sorties (see page 41) every day, one taking off at midnight, the other at noon. The routes were triangular in shape and 1,600 miles long. Much of the work was at low level, down to 100 ft above the wave tops. Every 50 miles observations of temperature, pressure, humidity, wind velocity, cloud cover and precipitation were taken and transmitted back to base on the hour. Although the aircraft were fitted with the latest navigational and radar

Supermarine Spitfire of 518 Squadron, Met Flight.

I Henderson Collection

equipment, crew comfort on these six-hour missions, in all weathers, left a lot to be desired. By the middle of 1946 the only Met unit in the UK was at Aldergrove. In October it was renumbered as 202 Squadron. The Halifaxes soldiered on until 1950, but not without cost, as four aircraft were lost while engaged on Met duties in the period 1946–47. The Halifax was replaced by another Handley Page product, the Hastings.

The end of the war also brought changes for 23 MU. Its first task was in sharp contrast to the restorative work it had carried out on many hundreds of aircraft – the storage and scrapping of aeroplanes which were now surplus to requirements. However, there were still other aircraft which needed repairs, maintenance and modification. Many of the new aircraft joining the RAF inventory made their way to Aldergrove in the late 1940s.

502 Squadron Re-formed

Another happy note was the re-formation of 502 Squadron in July 1946. Since leaving home in 1941 the squadron had served from bases in Cornwall, Wales and Scotland, gaining the right to display the following battle honours – Atlantic 1939–44, Channel and North Sea 1942–45, Bay of Biscay 1941–44, Dieppe 1942 and Baltic 1944–45. It achieved distinction on 30 November 1941 when a Whitley sank U-206 in the Bay of Biscay, the first ASV radar assisted sinking of the war. The squadron was officially credited with six U-boats destroyed, two of which were shared with the Royal Navy and other aircraft. Twelve other submarines were claimed as damaged, ten of these being shared with other aircraft. In addition, the squadron sank and damaged a considerable amount of

De Havilland Mosquito NF30 of 502 Squadron.

RAF Aldergrove

enemy shipping.

When the squadron disbanded at Stornaway in May 1945 it was equipped with Halifaxes. Its new aircraft was the famous DH Mosquito. Two variants of this most versatile of aeroplanes served with 502 – the B Mk25 light bomber and NF30 night fighter. Powered by twin Merlin engines, the Mosquito was constructed of cedar and balsa wood. It first flew in November 1940 and soon gave evidence of the astounding performance and manoeuvrability which made it the fastest operational aircraft in the world in the mid-war period. In all, 7,781 Mosquitoes were produced.

An Invitation to the Public

On Saturday 20 September 1947 the public were invited by "The Commanding Officer, Officers and Men of Royal Air Force Station, Aldergrove"[53] to attend an Air Display from 2.00 pm to 6.00 pm. Admission was free, with a car park charge of two shillings (10p). A programme could be purchased for "at least sixpence please" (two and a half pence), while for a further five shillings (25p), a boxing exhibition, weight lifting contest and "Dancing to the Music of the College Boys from 9 to 11.45pm" was provided. The star bill in the boxing was Rinty Monaghan, who the following year would become the flyweight champion of the world.

The flying display opened and closed with pleasure flights from Ulster Aviation Ltd. In between there was a varied programme – a fly past of 11 types of service aircraft, ranging from the Supermarine Sea Otter to the Avro Lincoln; several different flying demonstrations by the Mosquitoes of 502 Squadron and the Halifaxes of 202 Squadron; a "low level bombing attack" by three Airspeed Oxfords on "moving armoured cars"; displays from some Ulster Aviation Ltd aircraft, including the Miles Aerovan, Airspeed Consol and Miles Messenger, "with particular emphasis on the slow flying and landing qualities of the Messenger aircraft", the DH Vampire jet fighter; and formation flying by the Tiger Moths of the QUB Air Squadron. Moreover, there was also a comprehensive static display, including access to Stirling and Halifax aircraft. Ulster Aviation operated a fleet of five of the boxy Aerovans from Newtownards and was employed from 1947 to 1949 on tourist traffic to the Isle of Man and with a freight run to Woodley Aerodrome near Reading, taking Ards-built Miles Messenger and Gemini assemblies to the main factory.

In September 1948 502 Squadron, now a part of Fighter

Command, received the first of an even more famous aircraft, the Vickers Supermarine Spitfire. The F22 was the ultimate development of this supreme fighter. With a Rolls Royce Griffon engine, it had a top speed of 450 mph and an armament of four cannon. No fewer than 20,351 Spitfires were built between 1936 and 1948.

Civil Aviation Post-War

With the coming of peace, Railway Air Services, the dominant pre-war domestic carrier, lost no time in setting up a base at Belfast Harbour Airport, Sydenham, for services to London, Liverpool and (from 1946) Manchester. The Glasgow schedule was operated for RAS by Scottish Airways (formed in 1937 from the amalgamation of Northern and Scottish Airways with Highland Airways), who introduced the 20-passenger C-47A Dakota, when flying G-AGZA from Renfrew to Belfast on 13 May 1946. By a strange co-incidence, the pilot of that first Dakota, Captain Bill Baillie, received his conversion to type instruction from Nigel Pelly, the pipe-smoking pre-war Midland and Scottish pilot, who had attained the rank of Group Captain during the war and was to continue a distinguished career with BOAC. In charge of the operation at Renfrew was another very experienced pilot, Captain David Barclay.

The advent of the DC-3/C-47 was of significance, as it gave British domestic air transport its first aircraft equipped with adequate anti-icing protection. The aircraft was also larger, faster and could fly higher and so avoid much of the bad weather. This type, known familiarly as the Dakota, was the mainstay of British air transport in the post-war years. The sound of its two Pratt and Whitney Twin Wasp radial piston engines has been heard all round the world, in a multitude of roles in peace and war. The first of 10,926 DC-3s had flown in 1935 and it continues to fly in commercial service to this day – a career unparalleled in aviation history.

The Isle of Man and Prestwick were also served by Isle of Man Air Services and Scottish Airlines respectively. As previously noted, Belfast Harbour Airport had replaced the Ards Airport in March 1938, and though civil flying was greatly restricted during the war it had been the terminus for Associated Airways Joint Committee national communications links to Glasgow and Liverpool, which were extended to Croydon from November 1944. However, one of the consequences of the wartime airfield construction programme was the building of Nutts Corner, just three miles from Aldergrove. Because the airbase had been developed with large Coastal Command and USAAF cargo aircraft in mind, there were relatively long runways (6,000 ft, 4,800 ft and 3,700 ft in length) and concrete parking aprons available for the bigger commercial aircraft which were anticipated. Therefore, on 1 December 1946 Nutts Corner replaced Belfast Harbour as Northern Ireland's civil airport. Shortly afterwards British European Airways (BEA) came into being, along with the two other newly created government-owned corporations, the British Overseas Airways Corporation (BOAC) and British South American Airways (BSAA). BEA then assumed full responsibility for scheduled civil air transport in the United Kingdom.

The first non-stop service flown by BEA from Croydon to Belfast was on 20 March 1947 by the Junkers Ju52/3m G-AHOF. This was one of a fleet of these veteran tri-motors taken from Germany as war reparations and used briefly, without conspicuous success. (Ju52s had been operating on the Croydon–Liverpool–Belfast route since November 1946.) They had been constructed during the war to much lower standards than pre-war machines, in the realistic expectation of a much shorter active life. Another very unusual type, used between December 1946 and August 1947 by Scottish Airlines from Prestwick, was the four-engine, high winged, 22-seat, 1935 vintage Fokker FXXII G-AFZP, which must have made quite a sight in the orange and silver livery of the airline. On 19 May 1947 DC-3s replaced the Ju52s and the London terminal changed to Northolt.

Some of the early routes – which in 1947 included Liverpool, Manchester, the Isle of Man, Glasgow, Carlisle and Newcastle – were flown by BEA using the long-serving DH Rapides, as well as Avro Nineteens, another type inherited from RAS and a civil version of the famous Anson. (The Avro Nineteen has its own place in the aviation history of the province as the type which flew the first non-stop Belfast to London schedule, operated by RAS from Sydenham to Croydon on 3 December 1945.) Carlisle and Newcastle lasted only a few months as destinations, while Birmingham was added to the route structure in May 1950.

In September and October 1947, and again in the autumn of 1948, a considerable civil air operation took place. In response to severe milk shortages in England an airlift from Nutts Corner to Speke Airport in Liverpool and Squire's Gate, Blackpool, was organised. The milk was carried in ten-gallon churns by a variety of charter companies using Avro Yorks and Lancastrians, Handley Page Halifaxes and Haltons, Douglas Dakotas,

Consolidated Liberators and Miles Aerovans. At its peak, the 'Ulster Milk Lift' resulted in up to 30,000 gallons of milk a day being transported by air. There is no doubt that some of the skills learned on this operation were soon applied in the more testing circumstances of the Berlin Airlift.

Throughout the 1950s, Nutts Corner handled nearly all of the province's airline traffic. BEA successively used DC-3s (named the Pionair class, after being converted by Scottish Aviation at Prestwick to 32 passenger configuration, with built-in airstairs), Vickers Vikings (a tubby 36-seater based on the Wellington bomber), Airspeed Ambassadors and Vickers Viscounts to destinations in England, Scotland and the Isle of Man. The Viscount holds the distinction of being the world's first turboprop airliner, so offering a faster, smoother ride, G-AMOD initiating the all-first-class 47-seat 'Ulster Flyer' service to London Heathrow on 1 November 1953. The Vikings continued to operate to London Northolt for a further year. In 1956 Jersey–Belfast was added to the BEA route structure, using Pionairs. From the middle of the decade, BKS Air Transport provided services to Leeds/Bradford, starting in 1955, Edinburgh in 1956 and Newcastle from 1958, using Dakotas to begin with. In May 1956 Cambrian Airways began operating from Cardiff and Bristol to Belfast, with 17-passenger four-engine DH Herons, until in 1958 the service was suspended when the company experienced financial difficulties. Later, Silver City Airways flew from Blackpool, using DH Herons, DC-3s and Bristol Freighters. The same company also used the boxy Bristol from 1955 to 1957 on a car ferry service between Castle Kennedy (near Stranraer) and Newtownards (also flying from the Harbour Airport for a few months in 1956, while the runway at Ards was extended). Flights to RAF Woodvale and the Isle of Man were also offered from Ards for a brief period, during 1955–56.

International traffic from Nutts Corner, which began in the late 1950s, was all charter work. Amongst the types recorded in the spotting diary of enthusiast Bob Wilson, were Boeing Stratocruisers of BOAC, Douglas DC-6s in the livery of Pan Am and Capitol Airways, Lockheed Super Constellations of Seaboard and Western Airlines, Bristol Britannias of Canadian Pacific and, on one occasion, a Douglas DC-7C of Alitalia.

New Aircraft at Aldergrove

The early 1950s brought an influx of new aircraft types to all the units at Aldergrove, as well as the return of a former task, together with some dramatic record breaking and significant test flying.

In October 1950 the first specially modified Handley Page Hastings was delivered to 202 Squadron. This large four-engine aircraft, originally designed for transport

Handley Page Hastings of 202 Squadron.   *RAF Aldergrove*

duties, proved a great boon to the Met crews. It was much more roomy, with better heating, galley facilities and rest positions for off-duty crew members. The aircraft could also be used in a secondary transport role and were equipped with Lindholme emergency dinghy containers, for use on search and rescue missions.

The skill and endurance of the Met crews cannot be overestimated. A sortie, typical of many, has been recalled by Brian Mitchell, a Met observer from April 1950 to September 1951. The flights were known by the code name 'Bismuth', a word apparently picked at random during the war. (An alternative source for this has been suggested – Bismuth was the name of a contemporary brand of stomach powder and it may have been felt that a dose of this medicine may have been required after long hours over the Atlantic.) Mitchell's story runs as follows:

> Preparations for the flight begin the day previously. The Hastings is serviced and fuelled with 2600 gallons. Rations and survival equipment are loaded and checked. The navigator reports to the meteorological officer and works out the take-off time from preliminary forecast winds. The Central Forecasting Office at Dunstable decided whether the usual track is to be flown or a special sortie made. At 0715, we are awakened by the duty aircrew NCO. After a quick wash we climb into the aircrew coach, laden with flying clothing, diversion kit, log-books,

Brian Mitchell's Met Flight route.

thermos flasks, sandwiches and all the paraphernalia required for a ten hour flight. After a "flying meal" of eggs and bacon, we make our way to the control tower for met briefing. Today, as often happens, we will fly through a depression moving north-east, which we should meet about 400 miles out. This can mean ten hours of instrument flying in cloud, in clear blue skies and sunshine or a mixture of both. Unlike civil aircraft we must maintain our track no matter how bad the weather may be. Briefing over, we make our way to the aircraft. Equipment is stowed, engines are started and run up; there are no snags and we taxi to the duty runway. On receipt of a green light from the caravan, the engines are opened up and we thunder down the runway, becoming airborne at a speed of 110 knots. A gradual climb to safety height, 3500 feet, is made and course set for Donegal Bay – permission was given for all weather flights to fly over Eire. Soon the coast is reached, our last sight of land for the next nine hours. Apart from the occasional ship, we shall be alone, our only link that of radio. The met flight proper now begins with a descent to reporting height of 1500 feet. The met observer sits next to the pilot on the starboard side, he is the key crew member, as it depends on him whether the flight is successful or not. Around him is a comprehensive range of instruments but he also relies on his eyes for reporting cloud types and height, visibility, icing and unusual weather phenomena.

We are now about 200 miles out and it is time to descend to sea level. With all engines at full power we dive to within 100 feet of the surface. Even in the best of weather this is the time for precision flying; the sea seems very close, with grey Atlantic rollers rushing by the wing-tips. Today is really rough, with a forty knot wind blowing and waves about 30 feet high covered in white spume. The windscreen is covered with spray; the co-pilot stands behind reading our height off the radio altimeter: "100 feet...80...70...90...100." The met observer finishes his readings, gives "thumbs up" and with a pull back on the stick we once more climb to the comparative safety of 1500 feet. The information gathered is put into an international met code and sent by WT to Aldergrove, from where it is sent by teleprinter to Dunstable and widely relayed by radio and teleprinter networks, for the Atlantic is the breeding ground for nearly all our weather. We change course to due south and after a further 100 miles we begin the spiral climb to 18,000 feet. This is one of the most important points of the flight. We are now in the middle of a depression, rain drums on the aircraft, all lights are on and the bulky Hastings is tossed about like a cork. A complete set of observations is made every 1500 feet in the climb. We change course again to north-east and descend to sea level for the leg home. As the cloud breaks, we near the Pembroke coast, directly ahead is the Smalls Lighthouse; we are dead on track – no mean feat by the navigator. Another climb to 3500 feet enables us to clear Green One airway. Then we are over Belfast and a few minutes later, the wheels are rumbling down the runway at Aldergrove. The aircrew climb out, tired but conscious of a job well done and deriving some satisfaction from the knowledge of having helped in the work of forecasting tomorrow's weather.[54]

Aldergrove Enters the Jet Age

The year 1951 was the year of the jet for Northern Ireland and particularly for Aldergrove. Firstly, in January, 502 Squadron began to receive a new aircraft type, the de Havilland Vampire jet fighter. The Vampire, which flew for the first time in 1943, was developed just too late to see action in World War Two. It was a very distinctive shape, sitting low on the ground with a short, stubby fuselage and twin tail booms. The Vampire had the distinction of being the first fighter to have a top speed of over 500 mph. To provide dual-seat jet aircraft instruction, a Gloster Meteor T7 was added to the squadron's strength in May.

On 21 February another jet aircraft took off from Aldergrove – the English Electric Canberra WD932, crewed by Squadron Leader Callard, Flight Lieutenant

De Havilland Vampires of 502 Squadron. *RG Spencer*

Gloster Meteors of 502 Squadron. *RG Spencer*

Short SA4 Sperrin VX158 over Runway 35 in July 1955, with Shackletons of 120 Squadron on their dispersal pans. *Shorts*

Haskett and Flight Lieutenant Rolson. It landed at Gander, Newfoundland only four hours and 37 minutes later, having established a new record time, covering the 2,072 miles at an average speed of 449 mph. The Canberra was the first British jet bomber and has set an unparalleled record of front line service with the RAF. A version still flies in the photo-reconnaissance role to this day, 50 years after

the maiden flight of the prototype. It is worthy of note that most of the PR9 Canberras were constructed by Shorts in Belfast under sub-contract.

Another jet bomber took to the air for the first time on 10 August 1951. This was the four-engine Short SA4 Sperrin VX158, built in Belfast to fulfil Ministry of Supply specification B14/46 as an Avro Lincoln replacement and

Short SB4 Sherpa landing on Runway 35. *Shorts*

flown from Aldergrove because the runway at Sydenham was too short. But for the delay caused by having to reassemble the aircraft following its road journey from the city, it would have been the first British four-engine jet bomber to fly instead of the Vickers Valiant, which flew in May. The Sperrin was unusual in its design in that its engines were paired one above the other. Unfortunately, it did not win a production contract but the two prototypes (VX161 made its maiden flight from Aldergrove on 12 August 1952) gave useful service as flying test-beds for radar navigation and bombing systems. The contemporary edition of *Jane's All the World's Aircraft* stated: "Although the SA4 is unlikely to go into production, it does incorporate several important developments and ideas, particularly in construction and in connection with flying controls. It is fully capable of carrying the large load demanded by modern operational requirements."[52] Another Shorts aircraft to be flight-tested from Aldergrove at this period was the SB4 Sherpa, an experimental aircraft used for investigating the properties of advanced wing design.

On 31 August 1951 a Canberra again made the headlines. This time WD940, flown by Wing Commander Roland Beamont, beat the record set in February, with a time across the Atlantic from Aldergrove of four hours and 18 minutes. The next year, on 26 August, Beamont flew Canberra VX185 to Gander and back again in ten hours and three minutes – allowing for a refuelling stop – the time from Gander was an incredible three hours and 25 minutes. These record breaking feats were not Roland Beamont's only achievements – he also had a distinguished war record as a fighter pilot, flying Hawker Hurricanes, Typhoons and Tempests, achieving great success against V1 flying bombs.

English Electric B5 Canberra VX185 with 23 MU personnel. *RAF Aldergrove*

North American Sabre F4 XO725 and 23 MU personnel at Aldergrove.   *RAF Aldergrove*

Tours of duty as an operational development test pilot during the war resulted in a later career as one of the foremost British test pilots of the 1950s and 1960s – testing the Gloster Meteor, Canberra (making the first flight from Warton, Lancashire in May 1949), English Electric Lightning fighter (the first British production aircraft capable of Mach 2) and that victim of political expediency, the magnificent TSR2.

The Canberra's association with Northern Ireland did not end there, as Shorts were sub-contracted to build 132 B2s, B6s and PR9s. Moreover, many Canberras were serviced by 23 MU – the first of which passed through early in 1952. The MU was kept very busy during the 1950s handling Lincolns, Sabres, Shackletons, Swifts, Javelins, Hunters and Varsities. It also had the much sadder job of scrapping numerous surplus aircraft, including several Boeing Washington bombers – B29 Superfortresses, the same type that had dropped the atomic bomb – supplied to the RAF during the Cold War. The service's first home-produced nuclear bomber was the Vickers Valiant, some of which staged through Aldergrove on their way to the Pacific Ocean testing area at Christmas Island.

Coastal Command Again

Aldergrove became a maritime reconnaissance base again on 1 April 1952 with the arrival of 120 Squadron, which was equipped with the Avro Shackleton MR1 and which had been the first squadron to receive the aircraft the year before. The Shackleton was a direct descendant of the wartime Lancaster bomber and its successor, the Lincoln. It was powered by four Rolls Royce Griffon engines and carried a crew of ten – two pilots, two navigators, a flight

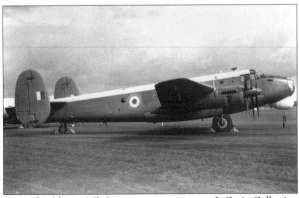

Avro Shackleton Mk I.   *L Craig Collection*

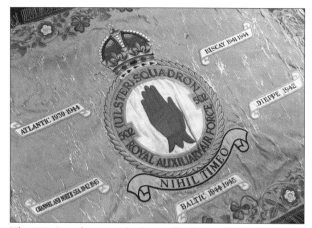

The 502 Squadron standard proudly displays its battle honours.

J Woods

engineer and five signallers, whose duties encompassed communications and detection of submerged and surface contacts. As well as routine patrols and training, the squadron was involved in regular exercises with the navy and was also tasked with search and rescue duties.

Another Royal occasion took place in July 1953, when a hand-polished, silver-grey Vickers Viking of the Queen's Flight, gleaming in a rare burst of Ulster sunshine, arrived with the newly crowned Queen Elizabeth II and the Duke of Edinburgh on an official visit to the province. They were met on alighting by a guard of honour and the Central Band of the RAF.

Sadly the sun was no longer to shine for 502, when, along with all the other Royal Auxiliary Air Force squadrons, it was disbanded after a government defence

Royal Air Force, Aldergrove, receives the Freedom of the City of Belfast in an impressive ceremony at the City Hall on 5 October 1957.

RAF Aldergrove

Saunders Roe Skeeter pictured at the Ards airfield. *T Maddock*

review. The last operational flight by the squadron had taken place on 10 March 1957, with a flypast by three Vampires over Aldergrove during the final parade. The Squadron standard, granted by Her Majesty the Queen, had been presented by the Governor of Northern Ireland during a ceremony at the airfield on 24 May 1954. On disbandment it was laid up in St Anne's Cathedral, Belfast, where it can be seen to this day.

A few months after the disbandment of 502 Squadron a happier event took place, when on 5 October 1957 RAF Aldergrove was granted the Freedom of the City of Belfast. A commemorative parade was held through the city to celebrate the award, which emphasised the links forged between the two over many years.

Also in that year a new service and new aircraft arrived in the shape of the Austers and Saunders Roe Skeeters of 13 Flight, 651 Squadron, Army Air Corps (AAC). The Auster AOP6 was a two/three-seat air observation and general purpose light aircraft, while the Skeeter was a small two-seat helicopter, designed to fulfil a similar role to the Auster. It was an important aircraft in that it pioneered the use of helicopters by the army. The AAC itself had been established on 1 September 1957, when the Air Observation Post squadrons of the RAF were transferred to the army.

In July 1957 the RAF introduced helicopter aviation in

Auster AOP6. *R Burrows Collection*

the shape of a flight of Bristol Sycamores of 275 Squadron for search and rescue (SAR) duties. In April 1959 this Flight became 118 Squadron. They were also used for border patrols and were greatly appreciated by the RUC. The Sycamore was used in a wide variety of roles by the RAF for twenty years, and while it was a limited machine by modern standards it provided good experience in the techniques of operating and maintaining rotary wing aircraft.

The first Shackleton MR3 received by 120 Squadron arrived in July 1958, replacing the MR2s which had been on strength for the previous two years. These improved

An Avro Shackleton Mk III of 120 Squadron 'peels off'.   *RAF Aldergrove*

versions of a much loved and reliable aircraft were held in high regard by the crews – though placing mats at the entrances, on which they were expected to wipe their feet before boarding, does seem a little excessive. On 1 April 1959, seven years to the day after arriving at Aldergrove, the Shackletons departed for the last time to their new base at Kinloss.

A Bristol Sycamore of 118 Squadron.   *R Burrows Collection*

Chapter 5

A New Civil Airport for Northern Ireland

A New Civil Airport

An article appeared in the *Belfast Telegraph* on 9 December 1958 headed 'Doubts on Airport'. Earlier that year the Ministry of Civil Aviation had decided to retain Nutts Corner as the civil airport, but the *Telegraph* was moved to comment:

> If Nutts Corner is not the best possible site, it is as well that the issue should be thrashed out before the £500,000 improvement scheme is far advanced. The local Aviation Advisory Council backed by British European Airways is pressing for reconsideration of the plan. It believes, apparently, that Aldergrove is the best site and that the provision of new buildings and other facilities at Nutts Corner is not putting first things first, since the runways there will not be adequate for the big jets of the future.[56]

The chief executive officer of BEA, Anthony Milward, gave his views at a press conference following a Council meeting: "Nutts Corner can never be an international airport. It can never be made big enough for the big jets and the Advisory Council feels that Northern Ireland should have an international airport."[57] When asked which airport would be a suitable alternative, he replied that the only one was Aldergrove.

A few months later, in April 1959, the chairman of Short Brothers, Rear Admiral Sir Matthew Slattery, entered the debate. He recommended strongly that Aldergrove should be developed for joint military and civilian use, with the proviso that Sydenham should be enhanced to act as a potential diversion airfield.

Two crashes at Nutts Corner may well have influenced the decision-making process. Firstly, on 23 October 1957, a BEA Viscount G-AOJA was destroyed with the loss of seven lives when overshooting, following a radar approach in bad weather. Secondly, another Viscount G-AOHN ran off the runway and was severely damaged on 13 April 1959, while attempting to land in a strong crosswind. Fortunately there were no fatalities.

Other options considered were Belfast Harbour Airport at Sydenham and the wartime airfields at Ballyhalbert, Bishops Court, Millisle, Long Kesh and Langford Lodge.

A decision was made on 29 July 1959, when it was announced at Westminster that Aldergrove had been selected. The local reaction was generally favourable, with the only doubts raised concerning the feasibility of sharing the site, and particularly Air Traffic Control, with the military.

Nutts Corner

Many of those who worked there have fond memories of Nutts Corner. It was by no means imposing or impressive, but the homely collection of red-roofed, whitewashed buildings was welcoming and friendly. Staff relationships were excellent across the board and there was a great feeling of belonging and teamwork. The canteen was the hub of conversation and news, where airport, airline and air traffic personnel mixed. Noel Russell started work there as an apprentice fitter in 1959 and by the time he retired as Belfast International's Operations Director in 1998, had become the longest serving employee. To his 39 years could be added another 31 from his father, who had been at Nutts Corner since 1946. He remembers a time when fewer people had cars. Staff and crew buses operated from outlying districts every day, while passengers who had their own vehicles were met by porters who parked or garaged these to await their return.

It was a much more deferential age, as another well-known figure on the Ulster travel scene, Maggie Gordon, remembers: "We didn't address a Captain or First Officer; we practically curtsied in their presence."[58] Technology was much more rudimentary – de-icing the runway was simply a question of shovelling sand off the back of a lorry, the radar equipment was housed in a mobile unit and poor visibility landings were aided by paraffin fuelled flares. These were lit by hand and placed in rows either side of the runway to act as a flarepath. The operation was not without hazard, as on the occasion when an over-enthusiastic

49

member of the ops team set the lorry carrying the flares on fire.

The Architect

In the spring of 1960, the *Belfast Newsletter* was able to reveal Aldergrove's preliminary cost estimates, which fortunately were comparable with the sum previously allocated to upgrading Nutts Corner. The article went on:

> The terminal building will probably be of the finger type design, similar to that at Gatwick Airport, which is the most modern in the British Isles. In such a design, a long arm stretches out into the aircraft apron making it possible for the aircraft to taxi along each side of it. A local architect Mr. W.H. McAlister is to design the terminal building (at a provisional cost of £150,000 to £200,000) but the Air Ministry Works Department will be responsible for the apron and taxiways.[59]

The Belfast Airport (Aldergrove) terminal building in 1964.
RW Huston Collection

The writer concludes with mention of another plan, which sadly never surfaced into the light of day: "The possibility of a direct railway link from the former G.N.R. station to the terminal building is at present under active consideration by the Ulster Transport Authority."[60]

Billy McAlister had first come to prominence locally in the late 1950s, as a result of architectural work on behalf of the carpet magnate Cyril Lord. He recalls that being given the commission to design the new airport came as something of a surprise. He was invited to a meeting in the Officers' Mess at Aldergrove, thinking that he was there for an interview from the various 'bowler hats', 'brass hats' and

'men from the ministry' there assembled, only to learn that he had already been selected. The party then piled into an impressive array of staff cars for a tour along the taxiways before he was asked, "Well Mr. McAlister, where would you like to put the terminal?"[61]

This was the start of a lifetime's involvement with what Billy McAlister describes today as the most fascinating and challenging work of his career. Now retired, the company which he founded, McAlister, Armstrong and Partners, has been involved with all the building developments at Aldergrove since the beginning. It was also the start of a specialist aviation role for the firm, which later designed the terminal at Teeside Airport and control towers at Liverpool, Gatwick, Sumburgh and the striking ziggurat at Aberdeen. He pays tribute to the great help he received from the commandant at Nutts Corner, Wing Commander John Selway, from the Ministry of Aviation and from the architectural firm which had designed Gatwick Airport – Yorke, Rosenberg and Mardell, whose services had been engaged as consultants.

By October 1961 the *Newsletter* was able to feature a photograph of a highly detailed model of the new terminal, complete with miniature BEA Vanguard, Viscount and Comet, as well as an Aer Lingus F27 on the apron. The costs had by then risen to an estimated £720,000. A Ministry of Civil Aviation spokesman was quoted thus: "Passengers may expect to benefit not only from the spacious and bright accommodation...but also from the fact that aircraft will be less liable to delays and diversions because Aldergrove's two runways of 6000 feet will be able to accept aircraft in wind conditions which at Nutts Corner would have made diversions necessary."[62] Assurances were also given that the new civil airport would be self-contained and entirely separate from the Royal Air Force Station on the other side of the site. Interestingly, the needs of spectators and waiting relatives were considered at an early stage: "On the first floor there will be an open air gallery, overlooking the apron, where passengers' friends and the public can view the arrival and departure of aircraft."[63] The national press, the BBC and UTV all gave extensive coverage to what was regarded as a very forward looking and exciting design.

The Political and Economic Background

By December 1962 another photograph, this time in the *Belfast Telegraph*, showed that the construction work was well in hand. The then Minister of Home Affairs, Brian

Faulkner, on a visit to view the works, commented favourably on the modern attributes of the building, but was rather more reticent on the subject of the apportionment of costs between Stormont and Westminster.

The architecturally radical and attractive design of the new terminal fitted in well with the mood of the time. In 1963 the new Prime Minister of Northern Ireland, Terence O'Neill, stated as his government's mission: "Our task will be literally to transform Ulster...to achieve it will demand bold and imaginative measures...to make Northern Ireland economically stronger and prosperous."[64] To this end, new industries were encouraged, with multi-national companies like Grundig, British Enkalon, ICI, Michelin and Goodyear given incentives to establish factories in the province. The new gateway at Aldergrove was regarded as an important contributing factor in enhancing the first impression given to potential investors and acting as an engine for growth.

The Last Air Display for 21 Years

The final Battle of Britain Air Display at RAF Aldergrove took place on 14 September 1963, just 12 days before the new civil airport opened. The highlights of the flying display were provided by the three V-Bombers – the Vickers Valiant, Handley Page Victor and Avro Vulcan – Hawker Hunter and English Electric Lightning fighters, a Fleet Air Arm Blackburn Buccaneer, several English Electric Canberras and a DH Comet. The weather conditions were just as good as the previous year, which had featured a mass take-off by nine Gloster Javelin all-weather fighters. Missing were the Sycamores of 118 Squadron, which had been disbanded in August 1962.

A View from BEA

As the main airline serving Northern Ireland, British European Airways (BEA) was heavily involved in the changeover from Nutts Corner to Aldergrove. Its house journal, *BEA Magazine*, gave extensive coverage to this story in its issues of October and November 1963. It is appropriate to quote extensively from these as an unparalleled contemporary feel is acquired. Firstly, we have an article entitled 'Last Flight Out' by the anonymous 'M':

> It didn't seem possible – but there it was in black and white, "From Thursday 26th September, all BEA flights serving Belfast will operate from the new civil airport at Aldergrove, sixteen miles west of the city. The newly designed civil airport and terminal will

replace that at Nutts Corner which BEA has used since 1947". The first year of operation saw 40,000 passengers – last year the figure was 575,000, from which it is immediately obvious that Nutts Corner was no longer adequate to cope with present day traffic. That such a stage was rapidly approaching had been apparent some four or five years earlier and after consultations with the Air Ministry and the inspection of various proposed sites, Aldergrove was selected.

The penultimate day at Nutts Corner, 25th September, dawned a bright one, thankfully and the transfer began. Van load after van load operating a shuttle service – desks, chairs, lockers, equipment both light and heavy, all were carefully stacked and dispatched and by lunchtime many of the offices had already acquired a forlorn and deserted look. Business, however, continued as usual. At the centre of it all was Station Superintendent Ralph Thurley. Going to Aldergrove will be for him a case of "this is where I came in" for it was there that he began his civil aviation career in 1934 with Railway Air Services. Sitting in his, by now, rather bare office, he commented, "You can't regret an improvement and that's exactly what this is. Nutts Corner has done its job and a good one it has been too. Tomorrow it's the turn of Aldergrove."

By this time the early morning blue sky had clouded over, the wind had dropped and there was a steady drizzle of rain. Almost within seconds, it had developed into a heavy downpour. Ralph Thurley, who knew his Nutts Corner, said, "This is all we need." He left me to see just how much the turn in the weather might affect the rest of the move for there was still much to go. Much of the equipment could not be shifted until after the departure of the last flight out at 10.45 pm and heavy rain combined with winding country lanes in darkness was, as Mr. Thurley so aptly put it "all we needed". Raincoats were donned, tarpaulins produced and the work went on.

By the late evening, the rain was little short of torrential adding to the general air of desertion outside. In the waiting room, however, there was plenty of activity and already passengers had arrived to check in for the last flight out. Not only passengers, for there were also quite a few of the staff, whose duty had finished, waiting about and staff had also come out from the Belfast office to send off the last aircraft from Nutts Corner. One of those was Jean Stanley, the long-serving secretary to the BEA Manager, Northern Ireland, from which post Robert Carter had recently retired. Jean commented, "I can't explain it – it's just that after so long...well I suppose that people will feel the same about Aldergrove ten years from now." To which Mr. Carter, who had first taken to the skies in 1917 as fighter pilot in the Royal Flying Corps, added, "Of course I'm sorry to see the end of Nutts Corner in a way, but we've grown out of it. I've been connected with Aldergrove since it first became obvious that we'd have to move, so for me it's the realisation come true of what was only a few notes on a piece of paper. It's going to be so much easier for the passengers, staff, in fact everybody."

In the distance could be heard the Vanguard from London, the aircraft to be (or so we thought) the last one out from Nutts Corner. [This was G-APEF, the 9.40 pm BE6062 service from London, to which reference is made in the signal below.] Suddenly, instead of the engine noise increasing, it began to fade and within a few seconds came the announcement over the tannoy that, due to the notorious crosswinds, the aircraft had been diverted to Aldergrove. There was after all to be no sentimental farewell, the last one to leave had already gone without ceremony, the reign of Nutts Corner was over.

Now the final stages of the move could be made and equipment held back for the last flight was already being loaded on vans within a few minutes of the diversion announcement. [Jim Logan, then a young traffic clerk but later to become the BA regional manager particularly remembers the long trains of baggage trucks being pulled along the winding country road between the two airports.] Passengers were transferred over to Aldergrove, where disembarkation of the first aircraft, several hours before any arrival was expected had gone very smoothly. There to greet this premature arrival was the new BEA Manager, Northern Ireland, John Swann, who had begun his career in aviation in 1936 with Northern and Scottish Airways at Renfrew.

He was full of enthusiasm for Aldergrove, "The new airport terminal building is functionally the best in Europe, if not the world for coping with the existing and developing traffic pattern. It has been specifically designed for handling heavy domestic air traffic demanding quick turn-arounds and high density airliners."

He read out a signal from Anthony Milward, the Chief Executive of BEA, "MY BEST WISHES TO YOU AND ALL YOUR STAFF ON THE MOVE TO ALDERGROVE THURSDAY stop YOU HAVE ALL ACHIEVED MIRACLES DURING THESE DIFFICULT YEARS AT NUTTS CORNER AND I KNOW HOW PLEASED YOU WILL BE TO HAVE A NEW AIRPORT WITH WHICH TO WORK."

A reply was sent in the early hours of 26th September, after the arrival of the first scheduled flight:

YOUR SIGNAL AND GOOD WISHES MUCH APPRECIATED BY US ALL stop NOW AT ALDERGROVE AND TRANSFER COMPLETED stop BE6062 DIVERTED HERE DUE WEATHER NUTTS CORNER stop ALL STAFF HAVE DONE A SPLENDID JOB stop VISCOUNT FROM MANCHESTER LANDED AT 00.16 HOURS AND VANGUARD FROM LONDON HAS JUST LANDED"[65]

It was time for 'M' to return by Vanguard to London, not on the last flight out of Nutts Corner as planned, but instead, the first departure from Aldergrove:

The engines were revving up and through the curtain of rain I could see the sizeable crowd waiting to see us off and within a matter of seconds we were underway. The lights from Aldergrove quickly faded from view and we were soon out of the bad weather and cruising smoothly through the night. The pilot of the aircraft, Captain A.J.B. Macreth was to provide the last coincidence of the trip. It seemed only fair that he should take the first aircraft out of Aldergrove, where, in 1931, he trained with the RAF as a Navigator/Air Gunner.[66]

Tom Grant Again

The Air Traffic Control Officer for the last flight from Nutts Corner and the first into Aldergrove was none other than the former young air gunner of 1938, Tom Grant. Later in the war he had trained as an Air Traffic Control (ATC) Officer under the command of Group Captain Jimmy Jeffs, the legendary 'father' of ATC, who had developed its theory and practice in the 1920s at the old London Airport, Croydon.

The first arrival at Aldergrove was at 23 minutes past 12 o'clock on the night of 26 September, BEA Viscount G-APIM from Manchester. This was followed at 1.20 am by BEA Vanguard G-APEH from Heathrow. The *Newsletter*'s air correspondent, NR Stockton, reported:

Early this morning, aboard a giant BEA Vanguard, I, with 100 other passengers, caught the first aerial glimpse of Ulster's new £800,000 skyport at Aldergrove. The clang of hammers, the whirring of electric drills, could still be heard in the building as finishing touches were put so that all will be ready for

Vickers Viscount. *S Finney*

Vickers Vanguard. *S Finney*

today's rush. Airline staffs were still installing traffic records, ticket facilities and office furniture.[67]

Some of the first travellers commented to the reporter:

> Mr. Leslie Mackie said, "I am inclined to believe that it has not been built sufficiently large to cope with expanding traffic." Miss Rosemary Wheeler added, "I feel rather sad at the change. Somehow Nutts Corner had come to mean home to me but I suppose we really needed something bigger than the huts." According to Mr. Thomas McClinton, "The two biggest improvements from my point of view are the finger arrangement which means we don't have to run three or four hundred yards through the rain and the fact that luggage is collected under cover."[68]

The first departure was at 07.09, the DH Heron G-ANCI of Mercury Airlines Ltd, which was returning to base at Manchester empty after bringing in a consignment of newspapers in the small hours. Other aircraft performing this nightly run were DC-3s of British United (CI) and Derby Airways. Just over an hour later, the first passenger departure was the Vanguard G-APEH going back to London.

The tower logbook for the first day of operations recorded a total of 53 aircraft arrivals and departures. The sole military aircraft was a Douglas C-117 12435 of the US Navy. This is of interest as it was one of 98 aircraft modified to 'Super DC-3' standard with swept wings, lengthened fuselage, enlarged tail and fully enclosed undercarriage. The most numerous aircraft that day were the four-engine turboprops, the Vickers Viscount, which could accommodate a maximum of 74 passengers and the larger 135 passenger Vickers Vanguard, both of which were to be

This was one of several C-117s to visit Aldergrove in support of the US Navy radio stations in Ulster. *L Thompson*

regular visitors to the airport for more than 30 years. A total of 445 Viscounts were built, making it Britain's most successful airliner.

Tom Grant had also been a party to the debate which had gone on in the 1960s concerning the future of ATC at the new airport, as to whether it should be under civil, military or joint jurisdiction. The civilian controllers at Nutts Corner had in fact been in charge of all traffic using Aldergrove, except for those on finals, just taking off or in the circuit. The military controllers' local expertise and experience was therefore much more restricted. For the first few months the RAF manned the visual positions while the civilians handled radar, zonal and approach control before assuming complete responsibility.

Aldergrove in Action

The second *BEA Magazine* article 'Aldergrove in Action' was written by Gillian Edwards:

> It was a dull late-October morning as Vanguard G-APEO taxied along one of the two new 6000 feet

runways and I had my first glimpse of Aldergrove. A few minutes later, the aircraft came to a standstill at No.6 bay. Engines were switched off, belongings collected and passengers disembarked. And it is, perhaps, from that viewpoint – as passengers – that it is best initially to describe Belfast's new airport.

Leaving the Vanguard, it was a mere 20 yards across the tarmac to the pier, through the gate and along the wood-walled corridor (which passes over a vehicle throughway connecting the two parts of the apron) to the waiting area. From here a staircase leads to the baggage claim area. By the time you reach here, your baggage has probably been taken from the aircraft and it is on its way by truck to be off-loaded onto a powered conveyor. At Aldergrove, the accent is certainly on maximum efficiency and speed. Everything has been considered from this angle. It is, of course, Ministry of Aviation property and was built under the direction of the Chief Staff Architect, R.S. Harvey. It has been designed to meet traffic requirements until 1968 and is capable of expansion when necessary.

My general overall impression of the building was one of airiness and lightness which is due to the huge plate glass windows, the sense of height which the unusual roof gives and the effective use of wood. Before designing the terminal building, the architects, W.H. McAlister & Partners, visited most of the recently built airports in Europe and incorporated the best features which would also meet the local traffic pattern needs.

The main part of the building has two floors; the lower one is the ticketing hall which passengers enter after alighting on a platform covered by a steel canopy, they then check-in or can buy their tickets. The general waiting area is on the first floor. To reach this you have to ascend the pillar supported staircase. Two opposite walls are just huge plate glass windows. The ceiling is not conventionally flat but instead is a series of zigzags, the profile followed by wooden slats set about two inches apart – most effective with the light filtering through. Facilities here are comfortable seating for waiting passengers, shops, snack-bar, an apron-side restaurant which can seat 180 people and a bar.

The pier, with six gates, extends to the customs area at the bottom, where two of the gates can be used for clearance of incoming international flights. Either side of the pier has engineering and apron service accommodation, which is a great improvement on Nutts Corner, where it was possible for aircraft to be as far as a quarter mile away from engineering headquarters – rather a long way to fetch something especially in bad weather. At Aldergrove it is a matter

of yards from either side of the pier to fetch a tool, minor replacement or whatever it may be from stores.

Behind the ground floor check-in desks are the BEA traffic offices, which control all aspects of a flight. Through the back from here is BEA's airside baggage sorting – only a few yards from the tarmac.

To the right of the terminal building are the continuing works, the cargo building, staff restaurant and flight kitchens. Until next spring, the staff can either take a bus across to RAF 23 MU, eat in the airport restaurant or bring a packed lunch.

Back to the ticketing hall, I had the chance to speak to the staff on duty. Ten of the desks are for BEA and the remainder used by other airlines conform to a very new, simple design. Ten desks means that passengers are dealt with quickly, efficiently and smoothly. Duty Officer, Mr. Bertie Hutchinson, a veteran of Railway Air Services, Belfast Harbour Airport and Nutts Corner, commented, "There are no major problems of operation, service to passengers has increased 100%. There are no queues because of the gate system. In fact passenger and baggage handling has improved a thousand fold, the latter because of the conveyor belt and covered baggage ramp. When I went on duty at Nutts Corner the first thing I did as I arrived was look at the wind sock. The crosswinds at Nutts Corner were notorious. If it was blowing in the wrong direction I then ordered coaches to stand by for a diversion. It's a lovely feeling not to have this worry."

The new airport has created a lot of general interest in Belfast itself and attracts a lot of visitors. From the restaurant they can get a close and detailed view of the aircraft on the apron – something not possible at Nutts Corner. There are other visitors to Aldergrove though. Nutts Corner was well known for the hares

Vickers Vanguard G-APEP.   *S Finney Collection*

resident there. RAF personnel stationed at Aldergrove say, quite seriously, that they too have switched operations to Aldergrove – that until the airlines moved there were no hares at the base.

It was time for me to return to London and as Vanguard G-APEP, guided by the new Ministry of Aviation Control Tower, taxied along for take-off, I remembered the staff eagerly looking to the future, whilst they remembered Monday, 28th October – the official opening by the Queen Mother.[69]

Royal Opening

The third extract is called 'Royal Opening' and was written by Dudley Fox:

It was a day of plumed hats and swords. Campaign medals pinned to well pressed pin-striped suits. A day for large bouquets and little girls, a day for ceremony, VIPs and spit and polish. Above all it was – as the Irish say – a "soft day" – in other words it poured with rain.

With royal promptness in most unregal weather, the all-red Heron of the Queen's Flight touched down from Heathrow at twenty-six and a half minutes past three o'clock and by careful timing, the pilot taxied away the necessary interval until he brought the royal aircraft to a halt on the rain-drenched apron right on the dot of 3.30 pm. His Excellency the Governor, resplendent in plumed hat, stepped forward to greet Her Majesty. Then a shy little girl in a pretty dress made her dainty curtsy as she presented an enormous bouquet and, her inhibitions forgotten, clung tightly to the hand of the Queen Mother. Twelve minutes and one Daimler circuit of the airport later, the royal party drew up outside the main entrance of the new air terminal.

During the morning preceding the royal arrival it was business as usual, though most of the five hundred BEA passengers passing through must have sensed the tell-tale air of preparation. On what other occasion would gardeners be laying turves in driving rain or would cleaners swoop on a cigarette butt before it touched the ground?

In the middle of the first floor departure lounge a red carpeted dais had been erected. In her speech, the Queen Mother referred to the 45 years of history at Aldergrove, one of the first aerodromes laid out in the United Kingdom, in the days when aircraft were made of canvas, wood and wire.

Standing on the apron were five gleaming silver turbo-prop airliners of the operators using the new Aldergrove – the most modern airport in Britain.

Informality was the keynote of Her Majesty's tour of the terminal. An unexpected call at the car hire desk caught the gent in charge telephone in hand. What does one do in the circumstances? Ring off, say pardon, stand up – or try to do all three at once? The Hertz man did just that and blushed into the bargain.

It was a fine day for Aldergrove to remember – the day the new Belfast Airport became a reality.[70]

The Queen Mother, with acting station superintendant TF Brown (left) and the Minister of Aviation Julian Amery, pictured in the check-in area during the official opening of the civil airport on 28 October 1963.

J Woods Collection

An aerial view of Belfast Airport in 1963.

Billy McAlister has special memories of the Queen Mother's visit. He remembers Her Majesty as being very charming but with a great eye for detail and with the capacity to ask searching questions. He presented the Queen Mother with a set of tweed car rugs, hand woven on a loom in the Mournes. He was later very honoured to receive a personal thank you letter saying that in all the presents that she received, this was one of the most practical, as she suffered from the cold when being driven to engagements.

In contrast, he was brought down to earth a little later by a telephone call from a lady demanding to know why milk shake machines had not been installed in the new terminal. She had been in the habit of taking her grandsons to Nutts Corner for a Sunday treat and was highly annoyed to find this lacking at Aldergrove. The omission was rectified.

Chapter 6

The 1960s

Commercial Services in the Early Years

All of the British airlines serving Northern Ireland in the 1960s have now vanished – some have merged with others, whilst others have gone out of business. Their names are evocative of a bygone age, their distinctive liveries but a memory. The aircraft were all propeller driven, either piston engine or turbo-prop. The open air spectators terrace on the roof of the boarding pier was the place for small boys (of whom the author was one) to thrill to the sound of screaming engines and the smell of high octane fuel. The sight of an Ambassador, its triple tail fins shuddering as the engines wound up to full power or experiencing the cacophony of a Vanguard, nosing into Gate 6, separated only by a thick glass screen, can never be forgotten. The

extension of viewing facilities along the pier took place during the first expansion of the terminal. In the beginning there was an open 'meeters and greeters' platform on the right hand corner of the terminal building.

The state corporation BEA, with its Viscounts and Vanguards, held sway on the main trunk routes to London Heathrow, Manchester, Birmingham and Glasgow, while also offering a summer service to the holiday island of Jersey. Cambrian Airways provided flights to the Isle of Man, Liverpool, Cardiff, and Bristol, using the smaller Vickers Viscount 700 series, with room for 47–63 people, depending on configuration. Cambrian had taken over the first two routes from BEA in the spring of 1963 and had re-opened the link to Wales and the West Country in April 1960. The airline was partially owned by BEA, which in 1964 also took a share in BKS Air Transport. BKS, whose

Vickers Viscount of Cambrian Airways.

P Cooper

Avro 748. *S Finney Collection*

odd name derived from the initials of its three founders – Messrs Barnby, Keegan and Stevens – flew to Leeds/Bradford, Newcastle, Dublin and Edinburgh, using 47-passenger Airspeed Ambassadors, 30-seat Douglas DC-3s and soon the twin turbo-prop Avro 748, which could carry 40. The Edinburgh service had been suspended in 1961 and was resumed on 11 May 1964, using the Ambassador G-ALZT.

Two companies which were part of the British United Airways group (which had absorbed Silver City Airways in 1962) – BU (CI) Airways and BU (Manx) Airways – provided services to Blackpool, Exeter, Bournemouth and the Isle of Man. A previous connection to the south coast had been operated by Air Safaris with Vickers Vikings on a Bournemouth–Dublin–Belfast route in 1961. The DC-3 was again to the fore, doubling up on early morning newspaper flights from Blackpool, with as many as five being used on a Saturday. Another BU(CI) type was the Handley Page Dart Herald, which was a 50-passenger aircraft. Like the Ambassador and the Fokker F27 Friendship, it had wings mounted high on the fuselage, so offering an uninterrupted view from its large windows.

The F27 was used by the Irish state airline, Aer Lingus, for the route to Dublin which had been re-introduced to Nutts Corner in the summer of 1961 after a gap of 13 years (a Dublin–Belfast–Liverpool schedule having been operated for a few months in 1947–48 using DC-3s and Vickers Vikings). Some of the flights carried on to Glasgow or Edinburgh. The airline also occasionally flew a very odd looking type on the service – the Aviation Traders ATL98 Carvair. This was a DC-4 converted for use as a car ferry, by the replacement of the original attractive Douglas nose section with a large structure grafted on, fitted with opening doors to admit vehicles. In passenger configuration, it had room for 66 people.

The original scene was completed by Derby Airways which used DC-3s from the old Derby Airport at

Fokker F27 of Aer Lingus. *J Patience*

The Bristol Britannia *Good Fortune.*   *S Finney Collection*

Burnaston, commencing flying to Nutts Corner in April 1962.

The hitherto unchallenged monopoly of BEA on the prestigious and profitable London Heathrow route ended with the introduction of competition on 4 November 1963, with the advent of a service by Harold Bamberg's British Eagle International Airlines, using ex-BOAC Bristol Britannia four-engine 124-seat turboprops, the first of which was G-AOVB. Both first and tourist class seating was offered, with great emphasis being put on in-flight service, including hot meals. In 1964, its only full year of operation, over 13,000 passengers were carried, but the licence restriction to a single return service a day proved to be uneconomic for the airline, which midway through the year replaced the graceful Britannias with Viscounts. After suspending services for most of 1965, operations ceased early in 1966.

Two Debuts and a Curtain Call

The opening month of 1964 also saw the arrival at the airport of a mighty aircraft on its maiden flight. On 5 January the Short SC5 Belfast freighter XR362 took off from the factory airfield at Sydenham and, flown by Short's chief test pilot, Denis Taylor, with co-pilot Peter Lowe and a crew of six, crossed Belfast Lough to Aldergrove. The first of ten, the largest aircraft ever built for the RAF, XR362 later became *Samson* of 10 Squadron and many years afterwards in 1977 was re-registered as G-BEPE, making the first revenue-earning flight as a civil freighter for TAC Heavylift on 15 March 1980.

In July the final 'Bismuth' weather reconnaissance flight by a HP Hastings of 202 Squadron took place, thus ending 14 years of continuous operations by this type. At the same time RAF Aldergrove transferred from Coastal Command to Maintenance Command, with 23 MU as the sole remaining major service function.

Another significant debut occurred on 14 August when

A Short Belfast makes a stately landing.   *Shorts*

Hawker Siddeley Trident of BEA.   *S Finney Collection*

British Midland Douglas DC-3.   *S Finney Collection*

G-ARPE, Aldergrove's first Hawker Siddeley Trident jet airliner arrived. European schedules from London had been started with this aircraft in the spring, but it would not enter regular service on the Heathrow–Belfast route until a few years into the future.

A Re-naming

Before changing its name, Derby Airways flew services from Aldergrove for a few months in 1964 to three destinations – Luton, Carlisle and St Angelo, Enniskillen. In all cases DC-3s were used. The first commercial service to St Angelo was on 13 March 1964, when the DC-3 G-AOFZ landed with a charter party of anglers from Kegworth. The first scheduled flight from Belfast to Enniskillen was on 20 July, using another Dakota, G-AOGZ. On 1 October, the airline became British Midland Airways (BMA) and as such continued with the Burnaston route over the winter of 1964–65. It also acquired Mercury Airlines of Manchester. As part of this deal BMA took on Mercury's station manager, Michael Bishop.

Burnaston was a grass field and was totally unsuitable for modern airline operation and so, on 1 April 1965, BMA transferred to the newly built East Midlands Airport at Castle Donington. The first service to Aldergrove on the opening day was with a DC-3, G-AOFZ, to be followed a week later by the inaugural turboprop on the route, Herald G-ASKK. A third type followed on 16 April – the Canadair C-4 Argonaut G-ALHY, which was a 70-passenger version of the Douglas DC-4, powered by four Merlin engines. The Argonauts and DC-3s also operated on cargo-only flights to East Midlands. British United staff initially undertook ground handling for the airline and also for Dan Air ad-hoc cargo flights. Geoff Menary, one of the British United staff involved, recalls a Dan Air Avro York arriving from Copenhagen with a consignment of pigs, which had to be

Canadair Argonaut of British Midland.   *S Finney Collection*

Airspeed Ambassador.   *S Finney Collection*

placed in quarantine. The Ministry of Agriculture also demanded that any handling staff should burn their shoes and socks, but this was indignantly refused. An Argonaut brought a single item of freight from Germany, a machine for Gallahers weighing two tons – this took some very

A Bristol Britannia in the colours of Caledonian Airways.   *S Finney Collection*

creative unloading, using a forklift truck driven slowly from Belfast to assist the task.

BKS added Teeside to its range of destinations on 12 April, the first flight being flown by Ambassador G-AMAC, which then continued to Dublin. This route was maintained for about 18 months.

On 13 August BOAC made a demonstration visit to the airport with the beautiful Vickers VC-10 G-ARVE. Its arrival was a promise of the potential of Aldergrove for services to North America. The *Belfast Newsletter* commented:

> Ulster's major airport is to have a future in the jet age after all. The 150 seat VC10 has made a proving flight to find out how the 6000 foot runways at Aldergrove can cope with one of the biggest jet airliners in the world. It is true that Boeing 707s and Douglas DC-8s cannot use Aldergrove but the VC10 is much more powerful. Last year Canadian Pacific, the company which operated a great many of the charters from Belfast in recent years decided to use Dublin, as they claimed their new DC-8s could not fly out of an airfield with only 6000 feet runways.[71]

While the VC-10 could indeed fly into and out of the airport, the take-off requirement with a full load of fuel and passengers did really require a longer runway to fly direct services to North America. In the meantime it was decided to provide connecting flights to the transatlantic airports at Prestwick and Shannon. Transatlantic 'affiliated charter' traffic was operated by several airlines, including the Bristol Britannias of Caledonian Airways, Transglobe Canadair CL44s and Saturn Airways' Douglas DC-7Cs. The affiliated charter scheme was a means whereby a sporting or social club or society could travel at a group discount rate. It was very popular, though perhaps not all the club members were as active as they could have been – tales of 'motorcycling grannies' belonging to TT clubs are doubtless exaggerated.

Northern Ireland's First Local Airline

Emerald Airways was formed by two Co Antrim businessmen – Mr W Scott of Toomebridge and Mr F McKeown of Ballymena. Route licences were obtained and two aircraft were leased – 17-passenger, fixed undercarriage, four-engine de Havilland Heron 1Bs. One of these was in fact the prototype G-ALZL, which had first flown in 1950. Operations commenced on 25 September 1965, the inaugural aircraft being Heron G-AOZN, with nine flights a week to Prestwick and (from 28 October) four to Shannon. One of the pilots was Mike Woodgate, who remembers the Heron as a delightful aircraft to fly. He wasn't as fond of the two Short Skyvans G-ATPF and

A de Havilland Heron operating for Emerald Airways.
S Finney Collection

Emerald Airways again, with a Short Skyvan. *S Finney Collection*

The perennial Douglas DC-3 Dakota. *B Gardiner*

G-ATPG, acquired in 1966. They were the early Series Two version of this robust and practical aircraft (which could trace its ancestry back to the Miles Aerovan) and were powered by the rather unsatisfactory Astazou engine. He was much more happy with the DC-3s EI-APB, -ARP, -APJ and G-AMWV, which came in following the purchase of 55% of the company by Hibernian Airlines of Dublin. This view is endorsed by another of the pilots, Bob Gardiner.

Further routes were established in 1966, from Londonderry (Eglinton) to Glasgow (Abbotsinch) and Belfast. The price of a single ticket from Belfast to Derry was £1 10s (£1.50). The first flight from Abbotsinch to Eglinton was flown using Heron G-ALZL on 16 September. Another scheme was the extension of the Prestwick–Belfast service to Enniskillen, offering short fishing breaks by Lough Erne.

The technical staff comprised three persons, for one of whom – Brian Boag – this was his first airline job. He recalls with pleasure the friendly, relaxed atmosphere at the airport – when changing the tyre on a DC-3, it was common enough practice to trundle it over to McCausland's car hire for a fill of air. He also has fond memories of the DH Heron – at one stage during the national seamen's strike, Emerald had as many as five of the type in operation, including the Mark 2Ds G-APRK and G-ARUA. Towards the end of 1966 he went on honeymoon and on his return was surprised to discover that the Skyvans had been replaced by DC-3s. The solid, reliable Dakotas were a pleasure to maintain. As part of a small team, Brian, despite being a licensed radio engineer, also had to turn his hand to engine fitter duties – and at times of need doubled up at the check-in. It was a great learning experience, particularly on a cold winter's morning when he worked on a DC-3 which had just returned from carrying lobsters, prawns and crayfish from Cork to Paris. Time was tight to re-configure the aircraft for passenger duties and to remove the smell of fish! Emerald also held a contract for radio work on visiting Constellations, DC-6s and DC-7s. The sight of a 'Connie' lifting off from the cross runway on a summer's evening for a transatlantic flight has lingered

A night-time picture of a British United BAC 1-11.

S Finney Collection

A de Havilland Comet operating for BEA.

J Logan Collection / BEA

long in Brian's aviation memories.

Sadly, despite much effort and expectation Emerald did not become the commercial success that had been hoped for and operations ceased on 15 November 1967. As for Mike Woodgate, he went back to flying instruction in England, but he will feature in this story later. Brian Boag is still active in local aviation, with his own avionics repair business at Ards.

The First Regular Scheduled Jet Service

The demise of British Eagle left the way open for British United Airways to apply for a London–Belfast route licence. This was successful, though to begin with only one flight a day was allowed. The service added a new destination to Aldergrove's route structure – London's second airport at Gatwick, which was BUA's home base. The first BAC 1-11 to arrive, on 4 January 1966, was G-ASJJ, which also proved a boon to the handling staff, as it was equipped with an auxiliary power unit for ground running. This 'Interjet' route was to prove popular with the travelling public, particularly as Gatwick had a very convenient terminal rail link to central London. The Northern Ireland manager for BUA was by then Geoff Menary, who feels that it could have made an even greater impact if several services a day had been introduced from the start and if an aircraft had night-stopped in Belfast, to

A Vickers Viscount of British United taxiing towards the terminal.

T Maddock

63

Another Vickers Viscount, seen on this occasion in the livery of BKS who used this type on the Leeds/Bradford service.

T Maddock

allow for the earliest possible morning departure. One peculiarity of the aircraft was a negative factor as far as sales were concerned – passengers were not keen on the rearward facing seats, which were demanded by the RAF in order for one of the 1-11s to operate a trooping contract between London and Germany. As an interim measure, BEA rose to the challenge with the introduction of the occasional DH Comet 4B to Heathrow. However, Aldergrove's runway was really too short for regular use by this type, a development of the ill-fated Comet 1, which in 1952 was the first jetliner in the world to enter service.

Other routes were being upgraded as well that year, with British United (CI) Airways re-commencing the Southampton and Exeter summer schedule on 1 April 1966, with Viscount G-AODG. (Southampton Airport had been opened again in September 1965 following the replacement of the original grass runway, with the result that the service had been transferred back from Bournemouth.) BKS also introduced the Viscount on the Leeds/Bradford run later in the year. A change to Scottish services was also effected with the opening of Glasgow Abbotsinch on 2 May 1966, replacing the old airport at Renfrew.

Also in the summer of 1966, Aldergrove greeted the Queen and Prince Philip as they arrived in an Andover of the Queen's Flight for a state visit to the province.

To crown a year which had seen a steady consolidation of the progress made since 1963, the airport topped one million passengers for the first time, and the terminal design was placed in the top ten of the Royal Institute of British Architects' awards for the best buildings completed in the UK within the preceding two years.

Jets in Competition

Despite the excellent qualities of the Vanguard as a robust, capacious and reliable aircraft, well-loved by aircrew and ground staff alike, it looked staid and unexciting when compared to the sleek and speedy BAC 1-11. Through no fault of its own, only 44 Vanguards were built and it failed to sell simply because it was unfashionable. BEA was forced to bring its own jet onto the London route and so introduced the Trident 1C with G-ARPC on 16 January 1967. In the first instance this was for the morning and evening flights only, with the trusty Vanguard operating the other seven daily flights each way.

The 1-11 and the Trident were the last wholly British jet airliners. Both were powered by Rolls Royce engines – the 100-passenger Trident had three Speys and the 79-seat 1-11 had two. Of the two aeroplanes, the 1-11 was the more commercially successful, with 232 sales of all versions. It

Hawker Siddeley Trident. *S Finney Collection*

British Midland Vickers Viscount G-ASED, introduced on the East Midlands service. *S Finney Collection*

Armstrong Whitworth Argosy. *S Finney Collection*

A Cambrian Airways Douglas DC-3. *S Finney Collection*

was still visiting Aldergrove in 1999. The Trident's production run stopped at 115 and it departed from the scene more than a decade before the 1-11. Though a solid, well-built machine, the Trident's design was too closely tailored to BEA's requirements, which limited its sales appeal. It also gained the nickname of 'The Gripper' – particularly on a wet runway, it was said to take-off only due to the curvature of the earth. One record created by the Trident has, however, lasted for over 30 years – a Trident 1C, flown by Captain John Welford, made the fastest chock to chock time between London and Belfast, taking only 39 minutes.

British Midland Airways enhanced the service on the East Midlands route on 21 February, with the introduction of the Viscount. The first schedule was flown by G-ASED, so starting an association of airline, route and aircraft type that was to last some 20 years. The first effect was to allow the frequency and capacity of the Belfast flights to be doubled.

BEA's dominance of the domestic air transport scene was further increased by the formation of British Air Services

Ltd, which resulted in both Cambrian and BKS becoming wholly owned subsidiaries of BEA.

The introduction of the Trident also brought about the arrival of another new type of aircraft, the Armstrong Whitworth Argosy freighter, for an all-cargo service between Belfast and London. The Trident did not have the enormous underfloor capacity of the versatile Vanguard and the Argosy had to make up the difference. It was a very distinctive aircraft with twin tail booms, a bulbous opening nose and clam shell doors to the rear. The seamen's strike of 1966 did nothing to harm the development of the air cargo market, while the transport of newspapers, now undertaken by Cambrian Airways from Liverpool, provided a steady source of income. The same airline also ran a general cargo service.

A third type of jet aircraft to make its debut at Aldergrove in the mid-1960s was the Boeing 707, when, on 10 July, Aer Lingus used EI-ANV for a charter flight to New York. Three days later Aer Lingus began a daily Viscount feeder service with EI-APD to the transatlantic departure point in the west of Ireland, Shannon Airport.

A classic shot of a Boeing 707 belonging to Aer Lingus.

Aer Lingus

Servisair vehicle and boarding stairs on duty. Since 1967
Servisair has provided ground handling for all types of aircraft.

J Woods

A final appearance was made by Ambassador G-AMAC on 31 October, when it operated the last passenger flight by the type for BKS on the BK624 service from Newcastle. Souvenirs of the occasion were presented to all those on board, including a pen and pencil set, a packet of cigarettes and, rather oddly, a vegetable dish. The Ambassador was still to be seen as a freighter on the twice-weekly schedule between Newcastle, Belfast and Leeds/Bradford, which began on 2 November.

On the ground Servisair Ltd came into being in 1967 and has remained a permanent fixture ever since, providing the ground handling services for those scheduled airlines without their own staff and for nearly all of the charter, newspaper, mail and freight flights.

According to the official end of year statistics for 1967, Aldergrove was the third busiest UK airport outside London, with 0.98 million passengers. In comparison, Heathrow dominated with 12 million, Gatwick had 1.9 million, Glasgow 1.5 million, Manchester 1.4 million, Birmingham 0.5 million and Prestwick 0.4 million.

Terminal Expansion

Since the very first week of operation there had been

complaints that the facilities provided at Aldergrove were not big enough. In September 1964 Billy McAlister had written an answer to critics in the Northern Ireland Tourist Board:

> I remember in a TV interview explaining that the terminal building was designed for expansion and that should it be necessary to provide this, the work could be put in hand quickly. The last few years have been a time of very rapid development in air transport and it was important that the original design should be capable of meeting this challenge. However it was necessary to know the specific nature that this expansion should take and this could only be done by allowing the building to function for a period of time. (Surely one year is a reasonable period.) The planning team are now very much aware of the necessity for expansion and plans are now in hand, based on the outline planned into the original design in 1960.[72]

A works programme costing £400,000 was started in 1966, with the result that by October of the following year two extra bays had been added to the terminal building, doubling the departure lounge and baggage areas,

increasing the size of the restaurant, providing eight more check-in desks and extra office accommodation, with the added bonus of a much improved spectators walkway. The flow of movement through the building was also improved, by segregating incoming from departing passengers. To this was added an extension to the BEA cargo terminal, which doubled the space available.

As well as experiencing a growth in passengers, the airport had also become quite an attraction for the casual visitor – an outing to the airport was a weekend treat for many an Ulster family of the time. The Lough Neagh restaurant provided a silver service meal and a fine view of the ramp and runway. Staff at that time have distinctive memories of their own canteen, situated at the start of what is today the location of the international pier – famed for its soda and sausage baps, as well as being the nerve centre for news and gossip. Brian Boag particularly appreciated the 'Greasy Spoon' after removing the last lingering traces of fish from the Emerald DC-3s.

More Big Jets and New Airlines

Though the runway was not long enough to allow for direct non-stop transatlantic services, both BOAC and Aer

The first Vickers VC-10 to operate a scheduled service from Aldergrove was G-ARVG of BOAC on 27 May 1968. Its passengers included the Prime Minister of Northern Ireland, Terence O'Neill. *S Boyd*

Two of the aircraft of Air Ulster: a Vickers Viscount (left) and a Douglas DC-3. *S Finney Collection*

Lingus were able to begin scheduled operations to New York, via Prestwick and Shannon respectively. Aer Lingus upstaged BOAC by four days, when its 707 EI-AMW departed on 23 May 1968, with a passenger list including the Lord Mayor of Belfast, Alderman William Geddis, followed on 27 May by the first twice-weekly VC-10. Not to be outdone and to highlight the prestige aspect, on board the first VC-10 G-ARVG was the Prime Minister of Northern Ireland, Terence O'Neill.

To begin with, the routing was London–Belfast–Prestwick–New York. Later, Belfast became the terminal point – the aircraft turned round there and did not operate through London. At the same time a feeder flight to Prestwick was maintained by the DC-3s, G-AMJU *Derry Maid* and G-AMWV *Ulster Maid* of Air Ulster, which had arisen from the ashes of Emerald Airways. The inaugural Air Ulster schedule had been flown by G-AMWV on 8 April 1968 to Glasgow. A service was also offered on the route Londonderry (RAF Ballykelly rather than Eglinton)–Glasgow–Edinburgh. During 1968 the airline also operated on behalf of British United on many Isle of

Man and Blackpool flights. Later, Air Ulster leased the Viscount EI-APD from Aer Lingus between July and November 1969. The former Emerald Airways captain Bob Gardiner also flew with Air Ulster after completing a stint with a specialised Bloodstock and Cargo Division of BKS, which was based at Aldergrove during 1968–69. Two Airspeed Ambassadors, G-ALZR and G-AMAD, were converted for the carriage of horses.

Another small airline, Autair, began operating for a time to Teeside (with its terminal designed by WH McAlister) and on to Hull (Brough), using HP Heralds. This aircraft type was also flown by British United Island Airways (BUIA) to Exeter, Southampton and Blackpool. BUIA was the new name for British United (CI) and British United (Manx). In the autumn BKS and Cambrian swopped two routes, with BKS henceforth serving Liverpool and Cambrian flying to Edinburgh. Before that, BKS had introduced the Bristol Britannia onto the Newcastle service, with the first flight being flown by G-APLL on 3 April.

On 19 June PH-DCD, the first DC-8, landed at the airport in the livery of Martinair, operating a charter from

A Handley Page Herald of Autair served the route to Teeside and Hull. *S Finney Collection*

Bristol Britannia of BKS. *S Finney Collection*

US aircrew pose for the camera after delivering three Phantoms to 23 MU from Cambert Field, St Louis, Missouri. *MOD*

Vancouver and completing the 6,000 mile journey ahead of schedule. The DC-8 was the Douglas four-engine rival to the Boeing 707 – a contest in which Boeing triumphed, with 1,007 sales of the 707 compared to 556 DC-8s. A few days later, on 22 June, a Boeing 707, N375WA of World Airways, made the first transatlantic jet flight under the banner of the Ulster Maple Leaf Club. This remarkable travel organisation, which introduced the concept of air travel to many Ulster people, had its origins in the Belfast Tradesmen's Social Club, founded in 1955 by James Murphy. Its first flight to New York had been in 1958 from Nutts Corner, 'hopping' across the Atlantic in an Argonaut in 23½ hours. Later destinations made available from Aldergrove included not only Toronto and New York, but also Los Angeles, Seattle, Orlando, Montreal and Vancouver. Aircraft used ranged from 707s and DC-8s to widebody DC-10s, Tristars and 747s. Perhaps the greatest benefit to be derived from the operation of Ulster Maple Leaf was the opportunity it gave to re-unite families and to allow far-flung relatives to meet for the first time.

Perhaps the most dramatic arrival of the year was on 20 July, when XT891, the first McDonnell Douglas F-4M Phantom fighter landed to receive the attention of 23 MU.

At this time the Phantom was one of the most potent military aircraft in the world and was the newest type on the RAF and RN inventories. After acceptance checks and modifications to ensure in-service compatibility, the same aircraft was the first to be delivered to 228 Operational Conversion Unit at RAF Coningsby on 23 August. Between 1968 and 1970 some 135 new Phantoms received the MU's attention.

Woodgate premises, formerly occupied by Emerald Airways.
S Finney Collection

Two of Woodgate Aviation's aircraft – the Piper Aztec (above) and Piper Cherokee (below).   *S Finney Collection*

Two New Activities

Within a few months of each other, two enduring aviation organisations were founded, which continue to function to the present day. The first of these was the Ulster Aviation Society, which held its inaugural meeting at Aldergrove on 15 December 1968. For over 30 years it has provided a focal point for aviation enthusiasts and historians within the province and beyond. It is undoubtedly the repository of an unrivalled store of knowledge on all aspects of aviation within Ulster, since the earliest days of Harry Ferguson and Lillian Bland.

The second of the organisations was Woodgate Aviation, created by the former Emerald Airways pilot Mike Woodgate, as Ulster's first air taxi company in April 1969. He began from a base at Stand 9 on the end of the pier, with two light aircraft, a twin-engine Piper Aztec G-ASFG and a single-engine Piper Cherokee G-ATWO. His brief was simple – he would fly anything, anywhere, provided it would fit into his aircraft and was within their radius of operation. He also offered more specialised flying training than could be provided by local flying clubs.

To begin with business was slow, but ironically it was the beginning of civil disturbances in the same year which began to put the company on a sound commercial footing. As the international media started to converge on the province, so it was that Woodgates was on hand to provide

Westland Bell Sioux AH-1.   *T Maddock*

The Westland Wessex – an aircraft that was to become a familiar sight in Ulster skies.   *RAF Aldergrove*

rapid transport. Mike Woodgate can well recall the feeling of great sadness that overwhelmed him as he took a film crew over the burning houses of Belfast. He also pays tribute to the great help and encouragement given to him by the airport commandant, John Selway.

The Military Build-up but Life Goes On

Another effect of the worsening security situation was a considerable increase in the number and diversity of service aircraft based at Aldergrove. At the beginning of the year, half a dozen Westland Bell 47G Sioux three-seat light utility helicopters of the 4th/7th Royal Dragoon Guards were all that was needed. As the year progressed they were joined by Westland Wessex, Westland Scout and more Sioux. An

Westland Scout.   *J Woods*

A de Havilland DHC-2 Beaver at Newtownards airfield. *T Maddock*

association began which has so far lasted over 30 years, with the arrival in August of XR523, a Westland Wessex HC2 of 72 Squadron, part of a detachment of helicopters forming the 'Ulster Flight'. They were first based at RAF Ballykelly from 14 July 1969, and when reinforced by three more Wessex the following month, moved to Aldergrove.

These rotary wing types were soon to be joined by a great Army Air Corps workhorse, the DHC-2 Beaver, a tough highwing monoplane much loved by 'bushpilots' worldwide. During the week of 15–21 August alone, no fewer than 144 Air Support Command missions were flown into Aldergrove, bringing 2,431 troops, 556 vehicles and 78,000 lbs of freight. There were 29 Argosy sorties, 29 Belfast, two Britannia, 79 Hercules, two Andover and three VC-10.

The military side of the airport now had rather altered chief functions – to act as an airhead for the secure movement of personnel, equipment, officials and VIPs and to become a base for active service Support Helicopter operations. Even in 1963 the idea of a major civil airport and a military base co-existing on the same site was viewed with concern – from this point on, the circumstances and the problems arising facing the airport's management were to be that much tougher.

Yet the normal routine continued. Aer Lingus and BOAC restarted the transatlantic routes after the winter break and the summer charter to Canada included Wardair and World Airways 707s, as well as Martinair Douglas DC-8s. On the European front Aeromaritime operated

BMA Vickers Viscount. *S Finney Collection*

piston-engine Douglas DC-6s on student charters to Paris, while Dan Air, Britannia Airways and Monarch Airlines flew DH Comets, BAC 1-11s and Bristol Britannias to sunny climes.

The local travel company Global announced in its summer brochure: "For many years our passengers from Northern Ireland have travelled by coach to join their flights at Dublin Airport. This year marks a breakthrough for we are now offering a series of two week holidays on the Spanish Costa Brava with a direct British Midland Viscount flight from Belfast Airport."[73] The inclusive package tour had arrived in Northern Ireland, from 29 April to 1 October, with prices starting at 50 guineas (£52.50).

Plans were also in hand to lengthen and re-surface the main runway in order to accommodate larger aircraft. The *Belfast Newsletter* asked the question, should Aldergrove remain as a compact terminal chiefly for domestic flights or should it expand into the big-time?

Chapter 7

The 1970s

Major Changes

On 26 March 1970 Brian Faulkner, the Minister of Development, announced at Stormont that legislation was being prepared for the transfer of the airport to local control. This should have taken place several years before, but had been delayed while protracted discussions took place concerning the precise financial terms of the deal. A few months later details of the £3 million plan to upgrade the airport were revealed. The most important work was the extension of the main runway by over 3,000 ft. The secondary runway was also to be improved and the landing aids modernised. Direct non-stop links with North America and the capability to receive 'Jumbo' jets would be provided. This was indeed forward looking, as the prototype Boeing 747 had made its maiden flight as recently as February 1969, while the McDonnell Douglas DC-10 and Lockheed Tristar took to the air for the first time in the second half of 1970.

Meanwhile at the airport itself Air Ulster ceased operations, BKS changed its name to Northeast Airlines and BUIA lost a letter to become British Island Airways (BIA), while also taking on the Prestwick feeder. Another change was that British United merged with Caledonian Airways (the original plan was for a take-over by BOAC, until Adam Thompson of Caledonian objected).

British Midland began limited jet services with BAC 1-11s to East Midlands (which also undertook 'IT' flights for

A Handley Page Herald of British Island Airways. *J Aitken*

BAC 1-11. *J Woods Collection*

A Vickers Viscount in front of the terminal building.
S Finney Collection

Hawker Siddeley Trident. *S Finney Collection*

The BAC 1-11 (left) and Vickers Merchantman, an all-cargo conversion of the Vanguard.   *S Finney Collection*

A spectacular shot of a Westland Wessex of 72 Squadron above the Carrick-a-rede rope bridge on the north Antrim coast.

RAF Aldergrove

Sud-Aviation SE210 Super Caravelle.   *S Finney*

Global to Majorca and the Costa Brava). The first revenue-earning flight by a British Midland-operated jet took place on the evening of 24 February, with the arrival of G-AXLL from Castle Donington.

BEA carried on with its mixture of Viscounts, Vanguards, Tridents and 1-11s to Glasgow, Birmingham, Manchester and London, although the airline also introduced an all-cargo conversion of the Vanguard, renamed the Merchantman.

Northern Ireland Airports Limited

The newly formed company took over operation of the airport on 1 June 1971 from the UK Department of Trade and Industry. It was a subsidiary of the Northern Ireland Transport Holding Company, which existed as a property owning company to provide funds to assist the province's transport network. Similar arrangements already existed to cover the bus and train systems. The shareholders were the Treasury and the Department of the Environment. The financial terms negotiated were very favourable, as the runways, buildings and services were transferred to the Holding Company free of charge. This allowed the airport to function free of any burden of initial debt.

The first airport director was already in position, having succeeded John Selway earlier that year. JD 'Dougie' Melrose was to hold that post for the next 12 years. Formerly a World War Two Lancaster pilot, he had been awarded the DFC and had subsequently been the director of Luton Airport. A man of strong opinions, who was not afraid to express them, his influence over the next decade in Aldergrove's history was to be immense. Perhaps the most crucial question of policy to be resolved was the nature of the airport within the Northern Ireland economy – was it to function chiefly as a public service or should it aim to be commercially competitive and profitable? Herein lay the seeds of much difficulty, since as a

quasi-governmental operation the airport was subject to much ministerial red tape and the somewhat Byzantine civil service financial allocation procedures.

Away from the Boardroom

However, all this lay in the future. Work on the runway extension was well in hand and events on the airfield over the year continued to develop promisingly. Nowhere looked brighter than the charter side, with the now usual big jet operations across the Atlantic and European services, with Air Spain Britannias, Caledonian/BUA 1-11s and Dan Air DH Comet 4s. The most intriguing route was that flown by Sterling Airways, using twin-engine Sud Aviation Caravelles to fly to Toronto and New York. The first of these classic early jetliners had flown in 1955. To save further development risk on a very innovative aircraft, the entire nose section and cockpit was that of the DH Comet, manufactured under licence. Sterling's 99-seat Super 12F Caravelles flew the Atlantic from Belfast via Keflavik in Iceland, where the passengers enjoyed a five-course meal during the stop over. The elegant Caravelle was to be a familiar sight in Ulster skies in the livery of more than one charter airline for more than a decade, the most prominent of which was to appear soon – the Spanish company Aviaco.

The Sterling operation in 1971 and 1972 was the culmination of five years of innovative activity by the Irish American Families Association (IAFA), which had been founded by Arthur Silver in 1967 as a group travel club. He had relatives in Toronto and found that the cheapest way to visit them was by arranging transatlantic travel for thousands of others. The first IAFA flight was in a Bristol Britannia of Lloyd International Airways in 1968, from Belfast to Toronto, for 58 guineas (£60.90) return. In 1969 and 1970, the DC-8s of Capitol Airways and Overseas National Airways were used for the main programme, while ad-hoc flights were provided by Martinair, British United and BOAC. The government changed the regulations in 1973, after which this form of charter business was no longer possible.

BEA also contributed something new, at this time, with the arrival on 1 July 1971 of the airport's first HS Trident 3B G-AWZD, which had a passenger capacity of 150.

The Runway is Opened for Business

Following the introduction of direct rule, the first Secretary of State for Northern Ireland, William Whitelaw, was appointed in March 1972. One of the happier duties he had to perform in the midst of a turbulent year was in October, when he arrived at Aldergrove in the Short Skyvan

A photograph which captures the elegance of the de Havilland Comet. *Dan Air Staff Association*

An Air Spain Bristol Britannia. *J Woods Collection*

Boeing 707 of BOAC. *S Finney Collection*

G-AZRY for the official opening of the extended and widened runway. The opportunity had also been taken to install new airfield ground and approach lighting. The occasion was graced by two Boeing 707s, G-APFJ of BOAC and G-AXRS of the recently renamed British Caledonian.

Sadly, there were no direct scheduled transatlantic flights to set the seal on the day, as both BOAC and Aer Lingus had stopped their big jet operation over the winter period. BOAC would not resume, but Aer Lingus continued scheduled services to New York and Boston via Shannon until 1974. However this could not take away from the fact that the airport now had the runway capacity to accept any aircraft then current or planned, exceeded by only a few airports anywhere in the British Isles. The Secretary of State promised that Aldergrove would be "developed to cope with demand and that the new runway will be matched by improved and up to date aircraft and passenger handling facilities".[74] Other factors were soon to divert minds and resources away from productive economic activity.

Car Bombs and Restricted Access

The grim events of 1973 were foreshadowed by the massive influx of troops and material in support of 'Operation Motorman', the army's effort to eradicate 'no-go' areas. For a period of 36 hours, in late July 1972, the activity at Aldergrove was so intense that an almost constant stream of C-130 Hercules transporters landed, unloaded and departed. In December 1972 the first of a new type of support helicopter commenced duties, XW215 a Westland Puma of 33 Squadron.

The security situation worsened and in the spring of 1973 the Provisional IRA declared the airport to be a "legitimate target". Car bombs and rocket attacks followed, fortunately without loss of life. The aim of the terrorists was to destroy the airport. In this they did not succeed, but massive disruption was caused. In order to ensure the security of staff and passengers as far as humanly possible, the terminal was closed to all except those working there, travelling or who were members of the security forces. Relatives and friends could come no further than the car park. An exhaustive manual search was made of all passengers and their luggage before they could enter the terminal. Check-in two hours in advance of departure became the accepted practice. Wooden and canvas structures were hastily erected to provide some rudimentary shelter from the Northern Ireland summer (normally wet).

A Puma of 230 Squadron at St Angelo airfield, Enniskillen.   *MOD*

During this very difficult and frightening period no praise can be too high for the staff and indeed for the majority of customers, who coped stoically and with generally good humour. Christmas and Easter were particularly fraught, with the careful and time-consuming examination of many articles, including well-wrapped packets of soda bread being 'smuggled' back to the mainland.

Operational problems were compounded by the unwillingness of some airline crews to remain overnight in the province, with the result that the early morning departures had to be flown over empty from Glasgow. Indeed, it has been said that on one occasion a captain requested an armoured car escort on the taxiway. The reply

has, perhaps fortunately, been lost to posterity.

Events in the Air

The year 1973 was also significant for the final appearance of several well known names. Firstly, the well-loved Vanguard was withdrawn from passenger service with BEA. Northeastern Airlines and Cambrian were wholly absorbed by the national carrier, the aircraft gradually repainted in BA livery, retaining only small company titling on the lower forward fuselage, until it too disappeared by 1976. Finally, the famous names of BEA and BOAC were replaced on 1 September by British Airways (BA), which pre-dated the formal final cessation of these two

One of the great military workhorses – the Lockheed C-130.

M Steenson

Three regular airport users and two familiar aircraft types were:

Top: Cambrian, with its Vickers Viscount.
J Woods Collection

Middle: Caledonian, with its BAC 1-11.
J Woods Collection

Bottom: British Midland, also with a Vickers Viscount.
M Steenson

Boeing 737-200 of the charter airline Britannia Airways.
M Steenson

corporations on 31 March 1974.

The effect on Aldergrove's new BA route structure was dramatic, with no less than 12 destinations now being served – Heathrow, Manchester, Birmingham, Newcastle, Liverpool, Leeds/Bradford, Isle of Man, Glasgow, Prestwick, Edinburgh, Bristol and Cardiff – using Viscounts, 1-11s and Tridents. The Prestwick service was operated between 1972 and 1976 by the chartered Cambrian Airways Viscount 700 series G-AMOG and G-AMON, fitted out in spacious fashion with only 54 seats and painted in the stylish BOAC livery until the merger. Sadly, the British Caledonian operation to Gatwick ceased, as the company was faced with a need to re-structure and cut costs, the last flight being flown by the BAC 1-11 G-AWWZ on 31 October 1974.

The next day the service was resumed by British Midland, using the faithful Viscount G-AZLT. This was BMA's third route, adding to the East Midlands and the Jersey summer schedule which had commenced on 19 May 1973 with another Viscount, G-BAPG. Another debut was made by charter airline Britannia Airways on 12 October 1973, with the arrival of the Boeing 737 G-AVRN – a type which was to become ubiquitous for the next 25 years (and beyond).

The following July the first wide-bodied passenger aircraft landed, a DC-10, N1031F of the American company Overseas National. This was by way of a trial run, as no passengers disembarked or boarded. In any case Aldergrove was not yet equipped with the necessary high-rise aircraft steps.

The Oil Crisis and a Near Tragedy

The international quadrupling of the cost of energy in 1974 was a heavy burden on the economies of the whole of the western world, but no region of the UK was more dependant on cheap oil than Northern Ireland. Reeling already from the effect of violence and terrorism, the local industrial base was hit hard by the inevitable sharp increase in the cost of transport and electricity generation. To this could be added the effects of the Ulster Workers' Council Strike in May 1974, which brought a fortnight of chaos to the province. It is again to the great credit of the airport staff that they weathered these storms. (An interesting arrival during this difficult period was a swing tailed CL-44 of Trans Meridian Air Cargo, with emergency generators and medical supplies.)

The optimism of the 1960s was now but a distant memory and, not surprisingly, passenger numbers failed to increase substantially until nearly the end of the decade.

On 23 July a loss of life of truly horrific proportions was averted, literally by a coat of paint. The Chief Constable of the RUC, Sir Jamie Flanagan, was among 84 passengers on board the lunchtime BA Trident flight to Heathrow. As the aircraft crossed the coast at Portaferry, a bomb warning was received and it was at once diverted to land at Manchester. A search revealed a device which, although the timing mechanism had activated, had failed to explode. This was because the drawing pin which was the final link in the detonator had not had its coloured coating removed, therefore acting as an insulator rather than as a conductor.

Wide-bodied Jets

It is therefore all to the credit of BA that the decision was taken to operate the Lockheed L-1011 Tristar (which could carry a maximum of 350 passengers) from London to Belfast. With the benefit of hindsight, this cannot be claimed to have been a great success. The Tristar was not really the most suitable type for the route, the volume of traffic on which was

Top: A Canadair CL-44 of Trans Meridian sits beneath a gloomy Aldergrove sky.
(*J Woods Collection*).

Bottom: A British Airways Lockheed L-1011 Tristar streaks into the blue.
(*M Steenson*).

more appropriate to a higher frequency, lower density mix of aircraft (much as provided by BA and BM today). The first revenue-earning arrival was on 1 July 1975 by G-BBAG, which brought 230 passengers and returned with 291. Jim Logan and Tony Moore, both now retired, well remember some of the problems created by the introduction of a larger aircraft to complicate the security procedures. Hand baggage was put into plastic bags at Heathrow to be given back to the passengers on arrival in Belfast. When faced with some 300 items encased in bin liners quite a scrum evolved, eventually leaving the staff amidst a sea of black plastic. The system worked a little better when see-through wrapping was introduced.

The first Russian jetliner to make a noisy entrance (and even louder take-off) was a TU-134A, YU-AJA of the Yugoslav airline Aviogenex, bringing a football team on 14 April. A more embarrassing landing was made by an Aviaco

DC-9, EC-CGQ on 25 May, mistaking the old wartime airfield of Langford Lodge, just a few miles closer to the Lough, for Aldergrove. Another arrival on 20 June was an Overseas National DC-10, this time N1032F and now able to embark passengers on a charter service to Los Angeles.

More Debuts

The start of the year 1976 brought an even noisier and more spectacularly performing Russian jet – the dramatically droop-winged TU-154A LZ-BTG of the Bulgarian carrier Balkan Airlines. It was soon followed in February by the arrival of a new face, Gerry Willis, as operations manager. Fresh from flying Canberras in Germany, he was no stranger to the airfield, as in the 1950s, when adjutant of 501 Squadron, he had visited Aldergrove in Meteors, Vampires and Harvards. Later, in the early 1960s, he had delivered

Tupolev TU-134.   *M Steenson*

Canberra B(I)6s to 23 MU. His first job was to wade through a mass of proposals concerning the long overdue upgrade and refurbishment of the services and facilities. His studies were interrupted by a mortar attack on the terminal building on 6 March, which resulted in the creation of only one access route to the airport and the establishment of a permanent vehicle checkpoint on the approach road.

By the time he became deputy director, in August, the way ahead was a little clearer. Stage one of a ten year £30 million development programme involved the extensive re-wiring of the entire site; major re-surfacing of the apron and taxiways; the provision of adequate primary generators, sub-stations and switchgear; a radical overhaul of the car parking facilities; and the construction of a much more salubrious primary search building. To this was added the very important bonus of becoming the first regional airport in the UK to be equipped with a Category III Instrument Landing System, allowing the airport to receive suitably fitted aircraft in the very worst weather. This work was all completed by 1980.

Woodgate's Prospers

During the 1970s Mike Woodgate's General Aviation (GA) business developed steadily. The North Sea oil boom ensured a steady flow of workers and spare parts to be taken

The year 1976 witnessed the Aldergrove debut of the Tupolev TU-154 of Balkan Airlines.   *S Boyd*

to Aberdeen and the Shetlands. The Isle of Man TT Races, and shuttling greyhounds and their owners to meetings, were regular earners. A more unusual incident that Mike Woodgate remembers was the day when 500 day-old chicks got loose in the cockpit of his Aztec. The work was diverse, fun and challenging – ranging in an area bordered by Helsinki, Unst, Rome and Lisbon. More aircraft were taken on short term lease, including the larger Piper Navajo Chieftains. The Pipers were ideal for the job, being cost effective, reliable and easy to fly, the Aztec in particular having a great load factor to range ratio.

In the late 1970s the company was awarded a nightly Royal Mail contract to Liverpool. Aerial photography and Air Ambulance duties were also added to the services offered. A local businessman used to maximise his time by the following regular schedule, all in one day – Belfast, Liverpool, Birmingham, Cardiff, Bristol, Dublin and Belfast, with an hour set aside for a meeting at each location. Aldergrove, with its 24 hour opening, suited the Woodgate "anywhere, any time" maxim very well.

The Shuttle

British Airways' great innovation of the 1970s was the Shuttle. This provided a guaranteed seat, without prior reservation, to any full-fare passenger who reported by a stated time, with a readiness to operate a back-up aircraft to carry those full-fare passengers, however few, who could not be accommodated on the first aircraft. The service was on a definitely 'no-frills' basis, with minimal cabin service. The Belfast–Heathrow launch was on 1 April 1977, with a Trident 3B, G-AWZG. What may be tall story, told by Gerry Willis, is that on day one, first in the queue to board was a man carrying a Lambeg drum, followed by a cycling team. Be that as it may, the Shuttle was a success, notching its first million passengers in the space of two years.

Aer Lingus also notched up a first on 3 July 1977, with the Boeing 747 EI-ASI *St Colmcille* beginning a short series of Maple Leaf charters to Toronto via Shannon. This was the first time a 'Jumbo' jet had operated from Aldergrove. Not to be outdone, British Midland introduced a jet to the Gatwick route on 12 September, the leased DC-9 *Darley Dale* OH-LYB. The flight time was thus reduced from one and a half hours to 55 minutes.

23 MU Closes but the Military Presence Continues

After 39 years and work on thousands of aircraft, 23 MU was closed in April 1978, following a round of defence cuts.

An Aer Lingus Boeing 747, *St Colmcille*, was the first 'Jumbo' to operate from Aldergrove. *M Steenson*

The last aircraft to be dispatched from the care of the Maintenance Unit was an English Electric Canberra, which departed for Luqa airbase in Malta on 1 February. The last recorded Phantom XV 573, had departed only a month before. The establishment had also made an important contribution to the local economy, employing up to 1,600 workers during the 1960s. Sadly, proposals to establish a commercial maintenance business on the site remained only pipe dreams and speculative newspaper reports. As a historic footnote, on 4 July 1977 the Vickers Varsity WF382, which had given valuable service as a station hack, departed to a sad final resting place – the fire dump at RAF Gatow. This was the last flight by this type in RAF hands and the end of a link to an earlier age, as the Varsity was the military version of the Viking, one of the mainstays of BEA in the 1950s.

The station of RAF Aldergrove was now a part of Strike Command and played host to an ever widening range of helicopters. By the end of the 1970s the Sioux was no longer part of the scene, but the regular Ulster Aviation Society survey in 1979 recorded no less than eight different helicopter types: Sea Kings and two marks of Wessex, HU5 and HAS 3, used by the Royal Navy (the first FAA unit to be based at Aldergrove since 774 Squadron in 1939–40 was a detachment of 845 Squadron Wessex HU5s in November 1977); Army Gazelles, Scouts and Lynx; while the RAF contributed a third version of the Wessex – the HC2, and the more modern Anglo-French Puma. The next type to depart from operational duties was the Westland Scout in October 1982.

It is worth noting that 72 Squadron, which transferred its permanent base to Aldergrove in 1981, did not confine its activities to purely military matters. The civil community

British Midland introduced the Douglas DC-9 on its Gatwick service in September 1977. *M Steenson*

benefited – especially isolated farms when cut off by winter snows. Moreover, a stand-by Search and Rescue (SAR) crew has been maintained over the years at 20 minute readiness to assist yachtsmen, climbers or divers, to name but a few. The most notable rescue was perhaps that of 9 December 1983, off Larne, when 80 passengers from the ferry *Antrim Princess* were airlifted to safety.

To round off the 1970s, a 'one of a kind' type passed through Aldergrove on 7 June 1979 on its way to the Paris Air Show. This was the 'Tri-Turbo Three' N23SA, a DC-3 converted to turbine power with three engines, one of which was located in an extended nose. A curious notion it may have been, but not a commercial success.

Opposite: Search and Rescue – a Westland Wessex on exercise with the RNLI. *RAF Aldergrove*

Chapter 8 — *The 1980s*

Reorganisation of Civil Air Routes

By 1980 the Viscount fleet operated by British Airways was in need of replacement. A decision was taken by the airline that instead of making the huge capital investment needed to re-equip the fleet, unprofitable routes would be dropped. Several of these directly concerned Aldergrove. The Liverpool and Isle of Man services had already been passed to British Midland in October 1978, while the small Scottish airline, Loganair, had commenced on the Prestwick route and some Edinburgh services in July 1979. Now British Island Airways (soon to be amalgamated with Air Wales and Air Anglia to form Air UK.) was to take over Leeds/Bradford, while Newcastle, Bristol and Cardiff

NLM Fokker F28.   *M Steenson*

A night-time shot of the Fokker F27 Friendship.   *M Steenson*

A Dan Air Hawker Siddeley 748.   *Dan Air Staff Association*

A Boeing 727 of Air Malta.
                        S Boyd

would be served by Dan Air.

Another major development was the first scheduled connection to a European city, which was started by NLM Cityhopper, a subsidiary of the Dutch national airline, KLM. April 1980 witnessed several firsts – the initial Air UK schedule to Leeds/Bradford on the first of the month, flown by the Fokker F27 Friendship G-BDVT; followed the next day by the Dan Air HS748, G-BEBA to Newcastle, Bristol and Cardiff; then on 8 April the NLM Fokker F28 Fellowship PH-CHD to Amsterdam. The year also witnessed the ending of the Aer Lingus Shannon feeder, which had been maintained with BAC 1-11s.

The establishment of a mail sorting office at Liverpool's Speke Airport in 1979 brought an increase in business to

Belfast the following year, when Northern Ireland was added to the growing Post Office night air mail system – the 'Spokes from Speke'. Spare capacity on the regular ABC Argosy freighters was used at first, before the increased volume of post resulted in contracts being given to Air UK and subsequently to Dan Air, Streamline Aviation and Woodgate Aviation.

The holiday and charter market was also providing a range of interesting visitors: Boeing 720s (shorter, lighter and cheaper 707s) of Air Malta; Boeing 727s (the more successful US rival to the Trident) from Air Portugal; and Transeuropa Caravelles, British Midland and Jersey European Airways' Viscounts to the Channel Islands. Boeing 737s began to feature more regularly at the start of

Spantax DC-8 at Aldergrove.   *M Steenson*

The majestic Boeing 747, seen here in the livery of Air Canada, was a regular on the transatlantic sector.   *M Steenson*

A Lockheed L-1011 of Air Canada.

M Steenson

the 1980s in the liveries of British Airtours, Britannia, Monarch, Dan Air and Air Malta. From Eastern Europe came the TU-154s and TU-134s of Balkan Airlines, Aviogenex and the Romanian airline Tarom.

More unusual arrivals were the Balkan Airlines turbo-prop Ilyushin IL18s (the Russian equivalent of the Bristol Britannia or Vickers Vanguard) and Convair 990 Coronados of the Spanish carrier Spantax, which was similar in appearance to the DC-8, but was designed to be the fastest jetliner of its time. The major presence on the European front was Aviaco with its DC-9s. The transatlantic sector was changing somewhat, with the formerly dominant Aer Lingus 707s and 747s being challenged by Air Canada, Wardair and CP Air, with 707s, DC-8s, 747s and DC-10s.

Tom Grant Retires

The year 1980 also saw the end of a long career in aviation, when Tom Grant left the Control Tower. In nearly 40 years in ATC he still remembered the moment which caused his most vivid 'heart in mouth' feeling, as having taken place on the ground rather then in the air. A young trainee had been asked to fire a signal flare from the balcony. The Verey pistol misfired and Tom can still see the face of the trainee looking straight down the barrel of a potentially lethal weapon to locate the problem.

On another day radar spotted a small echo approaching the airfield. Various frequencies were tried to no avail and down through the traffic onto the runway landed a Chipmunk, flown by a University cadet. He had been attending summer camp at Ballykelly when he got lost. He thought he had landed in Scotland and that Lough Neagh was the Irish Sea.

Tom appreciated the mix of aircraft that he had to handle: airliners, air taxies, light aircraft, helicopters and fast jets. The Phantom presented the greatest challenge, as an arrester wire had to be laid across the runway, which then had to be removed smartly before the next scheduled service landed.

Small Operators and Small Aircraft

Loganair, Air Ecosse, Spacegrand, Avair and Genair were all modest in size, if not in ambition, and during the early 1980s flew to a variety of destinations spurned by the larger airlines, including Aberdeen, Edinburgh, Prestwick, Blackpool, Teeside, Humberside and Dublin. They used

A favourite of the small operators was the de Havilland DHC-6 Twin Otter.

M Steenson

'cheap and cheerful' commuter aircraft, ranging from the diminutive Britten Norman Islander to its larger brother, the Trislander; from the Brazilian, Embraer Bandeirante to the Canadian DH Twin Otter; from the Piper Navajo Chieftain or Cessna 404 to the locally built Short 330. The capacity of the aircraft went from a handful in the Islander or Chieftain to 30 in the 330.

Two discarded services that were not 'picked up' by other carriers were the Air UK connections to Exeter and Southampton, both of which later re-emerged at Sydenham. Another fledgling airline, Manx Airlines, took over the British Midland routes to the Isle of Man and Liverpool on 1 November 1982. They did not really fit in with the 'International Gateway' image that the airport was trying to create. Herein lay the seeds of problems ahead.

Lear Fan

Following the closure of 23 MU, the government sought alternative industrial opportunities to utilise the skills and facilities available. The Lear Fan project was ultimately a failure, but it was a worthy effort. The aircraft was the final brainchild of Bill Lear, of Learjet fame. It was a revolutionary concept: a fuel efficient, high-speed, pusher propeller, eight-seat executive aircraft, made almost entirely from carbon composite material.

Over 1,000 jobs in Northern Ireland were projected by 1984, with the production to be based at Aldergrove. Delays in the certification of the prototype in the USA, due to technical difficulties, caused financial problems, which proved insurmountable. The plan collapsed before any local assembly or flying was achieved. All was not lost, however, as the factory and machinery in Newtownabbey was taken over by Shorts a few years later and formed the basis of their

development as a world leader in the manufactures of advanced aerospace composite structures.

Further Improvements

The second stage of the long term development programme, which was completed in 1983, saw both the main and secondary runways resurfaced; the completion of the dedicated international pier; the relocation of the check-in area to a new section added to the terminal, overlooking the ramp; a dedicated Shuttle Lounge; and the installation of the moving walkway, connecting the primary search area to the main passenger area. The search procedure was much improved with the introduction of 'Rapiscan' baggage scanning equipment. The airport was also renamed Belfast International.

Further evidence of the airport's increased prestige was the arrival of G-BIKB *Windsor Castle* on the 08.30 Shuttle from Heathrow on 9 February 1983. This was the first flight carrying fare-paying passengers made by a type entirely new to British Airways, the 195-seat Boeing 757. Two of those arriving in Belfast that morning were the chairman and the chief executive of BA, Sir John King and Colin Marshal respectively. On 28 May Concorde arrived in Belfast for the first time, in the form of G-BOAE of BA. It was there to take the lucky prizewinners of a *Belfast Telegraph* competition to Paris, including Ulster Aviation Society member Paul Martin. He noted that on take-off the aircraft accelerated from zero to 240 mph in 30 seconds and that the flight path was across the Irish Sea, past the Isle of Man, around Cornwall and on to Charles de Gaulle Airport, Paris. During the summer of that year British Midland offered transatlantic travel by Boeing 707 on a Manchester–Belfast–Toronto charter.

The Lear Fan 2100 preparing for a test flight at Stead Air Force Base, Reno, Nevada.

B Poots

Top: A Trident landing at Aldergrove during runway re-surfacing in 1982.

R Burrows

Middle: British Airways introduced the 195-seat Boeing 757 on to the Heathrow 'Shuttle' in February 1983.

M Steenson

Bottom: Concorde made its Belfast debut on 28 May 1983.

J Woods

In contrast to these high profile activities, the unspectacular but very useful nightly cargo work went on to the tune of more than 20,000 tonnes a year. It was divided into three main types: general freight, which was handled for many years by the Merchantmen of ABC Carriers; newspapers flown by ABC Argosies, Air UK Heralds and F27s, British Air Ferries Viscounts and Air Atlantique DC-3s; and Royal Mail services, using Air Ecosse Bandeirantes, Jersey European Twin Otters, Woodgate Pipers and Air UK Heralds. The scheduled passenger flights could also carry hold cargo.

Belfast Harbour Airport

A policy decision had been made to insist that all aircraft should be pushed back from their stand, but this did not suit the small operators whose aircraft could reverse by themselves. Nor did it suit their pockets to be charged for a service they did not need. Belfast Harbour Airport at Sydenham opened for business on 7 February 1983. From small beginnings it was to prove quite a headache for the new chief executive, Gerry Willis, who succeeded Dougie Melrose at the end of the year. Several of the little commuter operators opted to transfer their flights to the 'Harbour', including Loganair, Spacegrand, Manx, Avair and Genair.

The problem was compounded by the effects on the local economy of the worldwide recession, which saw the industrial base in Northern Ireland shrink drastically during the 1980s. However, it can be said that as the decade progressed, minds were concentrated at Aldergrove to face the difficulties, to improve the quality of service offered and to attract new customers.

Top: In March 1984 British Midland entered into direct competition with British Airways on the Heathrow service, operating the DC-9.

J Woods

Bottom: The Gatwick route vacated by BM was now taken over by Dan Air, using the BAC 1-11.

M Steenson

The Air Fair Spectacular of August 1984 included the Red Arrows in its list of attractions. *Belfast International Airport*

Diamond Service and the Super Shuttle

British Midland were given a licence to operate on the lucrative Heathrow route from 26 March 1984, thus providing a challenge to the monopoly enjoyed by BA/BEA for nearly 20 years, since the demise of British Eagle. The high standard of cabin service offered by BMA, using the smooth and comfortable DC-9 jets, was a major threat to BA's dominance. The inaugural flight was made by the DC-9 G-BMAI. BA's response was the 'Super Shuttle', which included the provision of a cooked breakfast on morning flights, a free bar and complimentary newspapers. The Gatwick route vacated by BMA was taken over by Dan Air with BAC 1-11s in February. Dan Air also extended its range of services to Teeside on 6 August 1984, replacing Genair's Belfast Harbour schedule after that airline's demise.

The 1980s also saw the emergence of a new force in civil air transport that was eventually to provide stern competition to the American aircraft manufactures Boeing, McDonnell Douglas and Lockheed. Airbus Industrie's first product, the A300, was a wide-bodied, twin-engine aeroplane, capable of carrying more than 350 passengers. The first example to operate into Aldergrove was owned by the Spanish national airline Iberia.

At the same time the international traffic picture was looking quite healthy, with an increase in passengers from 38,000 in 1976 to 300,000 in 1984.

On 17 August the airport hosted the first flying display to be held at the Aldergrove for 21 years, the 'Air Fair Spectacular', which included the Red Arrows, the RAF Falcons parachute team, an Avro Vulcan and Concorde in an impressive show. The philosophy of the airport at that time is well summed-up in the chief executive's introduction to the airshow programme: "We believe that Belfast International is here to serve the Ulster Public and we hope that we will create an interest in your local airport, which will bring you back time and time again; for we are aware that today's young spectators will be tomorrow's passengers."[75] The event was planned as a family day out for all, with any profits being donated to organisations benefiting the blind.

The last Trident to serve Belfast International Airport was G-AWZU.

J Woods

Farewell to the Trident

The year 1985 was notable for the swansong of the Trident, which had served on the London run for BEA and BA for 20 years. To mark this occasion, the Ulster Aviation Society chartered Trident 3B G-AWZU on 15 December for a one hour circuit of Ulster (nearly 60 years after the 502 Squadron Vimys). The flight passed over Belfast, along the lough shore, over the coast at Bangor, over Strangford to Downpatrick, then south-west to circle the Mournes, across country to the Fermanagh lakes, north-east to pass over the old airfield at Ballykelly, then via Coleraine and Ballymoney to land at Aldergrove, after the final low pass in salute.

The last scheduled Trident departed a fortnight later and was again G-AWZU. A solitary Trident 2E has been in place at the airport since February 1985. In common with many other Tridents around Britain, G-AVFE has provided useful, if inglorious, fire training service ever since.

A more muted last appearance had occurred in June, with the final flight of a Handley Page Herald in Air UK service, on a passenger schedule to Leeds/Bradford. The type was to continue on freighter duties for several more years, particularly with Channel Express.

Stage III Developments

The completion of the final part of the ten year plan in 1986 saw the international pier improved and a much needed extension to the cargo ramp. But the most dramatic change was to the main building, with the demolition of the original finger pier, which had simply become too small to handle the increase in passenger numbers and aircraft size. BA and BM (no longer BMA, having dropped the 'Airways' in 1985) were placed at each extremity of the terminal, with nose loading 'airbridges' so that passengers would no longer have to venture outdoors to progress from lounge to aircraft. In between and forward of the check-in hall, an eight-sided glass fronted structure provided more holding lounges and a viewing gallery for spectators, friends and relatives. This marked the final rehabilitation of the visitor to the airport, having been re-admitted on a limited basis since 1978. Atop the new edifice was an apron control room, giving airside operations an excellent vantage point.

As well as these tangible improvements, the Operations

Malinair, using the Britten Norman Islander, provided flights to Aberdeen and Glasgow.

M Steenson

Top: The Dornier 228 was the other main aircraft operated by Malinair.

M Steenson

Bottom: By contrast, this sleek Douglas DC-8 was chartered from Surinam Airways for use on the London route.

M Steenson

Department was reorganised and new training courses were introduced. Emergency provision was enhanced, not only by paper exercises but also by the development of a 'live play' annual training exercise, which involved all the emergency services and support organisations. Motorised equipment was also updated, including new vehicles for fire-fighting as well as snow and ice clearance. A further initiative that year was the production of a free monthly news magazine, *Skylines*. Sadly, this excellent and informative production lasted only a few months and copies are now collectors' items.

A sign that management had realised the need to encourage the small airline, was the provision of services by Malinair to Aberdeen and Glasgow, using firstly Islanders

and then Dornier 228s. Surprise arrivals during the year included, on 4 September, a Russian Ilyushin IL62 (the Soviet version of the VC-10) making a re-fuelling stop on its Moscow to Havana route, a task normally carried out at Shannon which was fogbound on this occasion. Even more dramatic, for a lucky few, was the appearance of Concorde on the Shuttle. This happened now and again, when a supersonic charter would otherwise have returned to base empty. Other one-off oddities to London, replacing the usual 757s in early 1987, were a BA 747 and a DC-8 chartered from Surinam Airways. Another rarity was the Bristol Freighter G-BISU belonging to Air Atlantique which appeared on the newspaper run. The Summer IT programme looked very healthy, with 16 airlines flying to

25 destinations, using 14 different types of aircraft from Caravelles and Viscounts to Boeings, large and small, and including a new Airbus, the A310, the smaller brother of the A300.

A second Air Fair was held on 22 August 1987. It aimed to be bigger and better than the first and provided six hours of non-stop aerial activity, while the normal civil and military traffic continued to function. The end of the year also saw a departure. Whatever problems he faced in his four years in charge, it can be fairly said of Gerry Willis that as chief executive he was imaginative and innovative. He made every effort to promote and market the airport to the widest possible audience and to broaden its appeal, typified by the slogan, "a nice place to come home to". His leaving was regretted by many. During his final year in charge, passenger numbers passed the two million a year mark for the first time.

More New Building and New Types

During the course of the year an Executive Aviation Terminal was opened, with the airport being marketed to the operators of business jets as the most westerly airport in

Top: TNT – the carrier with the alarming name – used the BAe 146.

M Steenson

Bottom: British Midland further upgraded its service to London by introducing the Boeing 737.

J Woods

the UK with full Category III landing capability. It was hoped that transatlantic custom wishing to make technical and re-fuelling stops would chose Aldergrove. A full range of services was provided including customs/immigration facilities, in-flight catering, lounge and crew rest area. At the same time a Business Centre was opened offering conference space for up to 120 people, two boardrooms and a smaller interview room. Full office and secretarial services were offered, as well as catering facilities. There is no doubt that these were imaginative and attractive ventures, but over the years they have failed to develop as strongly as would have been wished. Marketing a positive image of Northern Ireland worldwide has not been easy.

However, British Midland showed continuing confidence by introducing two new types of aircraft. The 737-300, a 149-seat version of the 'Baby Boeing', nearly 4,000 of which have been sold since its debut as the 737-100 in 1967, came onto the Heathrow route, G-OBMA and G-OBMB, quickly proving popular. The BAe Advanced Turboprop (ATP) G-BMYK arrived from East Midlands towards the end of the year, a much enhanced development of the HS748. It failed to sell in large numbers despite being a sturdy and economical design. Another British newcomer, the BAe 146-200QT G-TNTA, one of the quietest jetliners ever built, began to operate on cargo services for the parcel carrier TNT. The first mention of this company a few years earlier, in connection with hold freight onboard an ABC Carriers aircraft, had caused the Servisair duty officer a few palpitations. More than a decade afterwards, and now the station manager, Ronnie McClune still remembers being a little taken aback by the announcement of TNT on the next flight.

Further Shannon diversions included an Ilyushin IL86, the Russian 'Airbus', and the Ilyushin IL76 freighter, with its distinctive military style glazed nose. The cargo ramp was also graced by the presence of EI-BNO, the unique Heavylift CL-44-O 'Guppy' with a load of cars for the Ulster Motor Show. This odd looking aircraft, also known as the 'Skymonster', was converted to have an outsize bulbous fuselage. A more prosaic DC-3 brought in a Williams Formula 1 racing car, which was re-assembled by two mechanics in the baggage bay below the terminal.

Sadly, Malinair ceased services during 1988 and another small company, Iona National Airways, found it hard to make the Dublin connection profitable.

In the same year British Midland further increased their capacity to London by introducing the then top of the range 737, the 168 passenger 400 series, G-OBME and

G-OBMF. Another boost was the start of a scheduled service to Paris by TAT, a subsidiary of Air France, using Fokker F28s, with the first flight, on 31 October, undertaken by F-GBBX. On the still booming IT charter side the McDonnell Douglas MD83s of Spanair began to appear, these being a stretched and extensively modernised development of the familiar DC-9.

Kegworth

On 8 January 1989 the British Midland 737-400 G-OBME, en route from London to Belfast on the evening BD92 service, developed engine problems which resulted in an attempted emergency landing at East Midlands Airport. Tragically, the aircraft just failed to reach the runway and instead impacted on an embankment at the verge of the M1 motorway at Kegworth. Forty-seven people were killed and 78 injured. The effect of this disaster on the airport and airline staff can still be felt to this day. In a relatively small country and even with its recent troubled past, the loss of so many familiar faces affected those involved very deeply. Many of the passengers were frequent travellers and were well known at the airport. They had shown great loyalty to the airline over the years, as it had grown from small beginnings, and in turn the staff felt a great duty of care to them. The BM staff remember that night and the subsequent days with great clarity, and pay tribute to the offers of help which flooded in from other airlines, the local travel trade and especially the airport management.

The Return of 'BEA'

During the course of 1989 British Airways began to turn to other operators to provide some of the Birmingham schedules on its behalf. One of these was Aberdeen Airways with a type more normally used as a corporate transport,

An Airbus A320 of British Airways.   *J Woods*

Three photographs which demonstrate the wide variety of aircraft encountered at Aldergrove:

Top: A Boeing 737-200 of Britannia Airways.

M Steenson

Middle: A Britten Norman Islander of the Army Air Corps.

J Woods

Bottom: A Boeing Chinook of 7 Squadron.

J Woods

the Grumman Gulfstream 1, G-BRWW. Of greater significance were the leased Fokker 50s OY-MMU and -MMV of Birmingham Executive Aviation, which became Birmingham European Airways – thus bringing 'BEA' back to Aldergrove from May onwards.

A couple of months earlier, on 2 March, a Dan Air HS 748 G-BFLL, on the DA141 service from Newcastle, had made a rather more embarrassing arrival, when it landed with 29 passengers on board at Langford Lodge by mistake. This was before the establishment of the museum by the Ulster Aviation Society there, which was perhaps fortunate for the airline, as some of the enthusiastic members may have wished to add the 748 to the Society's aircraft collection. As it was, the passengers proceeded to Aldergrove by bus, while the aircraft flew out empty.

An important type which made its debut at the airport on a training flight on 26 June was the Airbus A320 G-BUSB of British Airways. This 149-seat, fly-by-wire, narrowbody was to prove highly successful commercially in direct competition with the Boeing 737 and the McDonnell Douglas MD80 series. On 8 December

Britannia Airways, which was much better known for holiday charter flights, began a scheduled service to Luton using 737s, with a very attractive fare of £29 single.

The military side of Aldergrove saw a sad farewell to the reliable and distinctive Beavers of the Army Air Corps, the final flypast being made by XP769 and XP825 on 18 June. Their role as the fixed-wing element of army flying was taken over by the Britten-Norman Islander, one of the most successful aircraft designed in Britain since the war, with over 1,300 having been produced since 1965. The first army Islander AL1, ZG846 had arrived at Aldergrove on 10 March, a flight of five aircraft being formed. A noisier contribution to the aviation scene was made regularly by the giant twin-rotor Chinooks, on detachment from 7 Squadron.

Another familiar fixture to retire in 1989 was Mike Woodgate. He offered his managers the chance to buy him out, with the result that several smaller but related units were formed covering the fields of air charter, flight training, aircraft maintenance and the sales and servicing of electronic components.

Chapter
9
The 1990s

The Hawker Siddeley 748, used by BA on its Glasgow service.

M Steenson

More New Building and BEA Makes Progress

Further construction was begun in 1990 with the start of work on a new cargo centre, while the East Terminal Extension gave upgraded and improved passenger facilities. Both BA and BM were provided with new, enlarged departure lounges, BM also gaining a new check-in. A more modern and spacious baggage reclaim area was added and the departures concourse was extended, as was the viewing gallery. The project lasted some 16 months and was divided into 14 separate phases, to ensure that the disruption to airport operations was kept to the minimum.

In the air, Birmingham European introduced 1-11s, while Britannia supplemented the regular 737s with larger 757s (longer) and 767s (fatter). BA replaced the 748 on the Glasgow run with the more modern ATP. The last BA service to Birmingham was on 27 October, using the 1-11 G-AWYS and the Air France/TAT Paris schedule ceased on 29 December.

Charter traffic was dominated by 737s and 757s, with the occasional Tristar, DC-9, MD83, 1-11 or TU-154. The main carriers were Air Europa, British Midland, Inter European, Viva, American Trans Air and Air Transat. In March Air France featured in a special charter for the *Belfast Telegraph*, using the BAe Concorde F-BTSC.

Top: The BAe ATP was introduced by BA to take the place of the HS 748 on the Glasgow route.

J Woods

Bottom: The ill-fated Air France Concorde F-BTSC, which crashed outside Charles de Gaulle Airport on 25 July 2000, seen here on a happier occasion, taking passengers on board for a special *Belfast Telegraph* charter from Aldergrove in March 1990.

Belfast International Airport

Arrivals and Departures

On 8 April 1991 Dan Air HS748, G-BIUV flew the last Newcastle–Belfast–Cardiff–Bristol–Belfast–Newcastle route rotation. The airline was facing a need to re-structure for financial reasons. The Newcastle connection was maintained by a new small company Gill Air, with Shorts 330s and 360s. Bristol and Cardiff were lost to the City

Airport. The serious nature of the challenge offered by Belfast City Airport can be gauged from the International Airport's Annual Report:

> Northern Ireland is unique in Europe in having a population base of 1.5 million served by two substantial airports within 20 miles of each other. This has serious implications on the future

development of airport facilities. The frequent response to this situation is that competition brings more air services and better facilities to the passenger. That may well be so in large catchment areas such as London, Paris and Manchester. But it is not so in a small region like Northern Ireland where the very high cost of airport infrastructure and limited resources available will act against the consumers' long term interests if there is duplication of facilities.[76]

Some good news came at the end of the year, with the re-establishment of the Paris link on 1 November by British Midland, using DC-9s.

The New Cargo Terminal

The cargo centre was officially opened on 17 July 1991. It was designed to offer the user a fully integrated range of freight handling services with an extensive, dedicated aircraft apron, adjacent terminal, freight yard, handling agents, customs brokers, forwarding agents and express transport operators all co-located on the same site. Its worth was to be seen early in the following year, with the formation of the Post Office Skynet next-day mail distribution system, which reorganised the existing postal network and saw Belfast connected nightly with Liverpool, East Midlands, Stansted, Bristol and Edinburgh.

Later in the year Birmingham European merged with Brymon Airways to become Brymon European. The Birmingham route was now serviced by a mixture of 1-11s,

the quiet twin-engine Canadian turboprop, the DHC Dash 8, its four-engine stablemate the DHC-7 and, at off-peak times, the 19 passenger BAe Jetstream 31. This smaller aircraft was also used on a short-lived new service to Humberside.

The ending of the Dan Air connection came with the cessation of the Gatwick service in November 1992. The eight years of operation had been provided mostly by 1-11s, supplemented by BAe 146s and occasional Boeing 727s. Sadly it also saw the end of this airline which had been part of the British aviation scene since 1953, when it was founded by Messrs Davies and Newman (hence the DAN). It was wholly absorbed by BA. So was broken the very useful alternative London connection which had been provided by British United/British Caledonian, British Midland and Dan Air since 1966. Jersey European filled the breach from April 1993, but used the City Airport.

A new operator appeared on the military side of the field, when the Royal Ulster Constabulary commenced operations with its Britten-Norman BN-2T Islander G-BSWR. In addition to supplying air support to the police, the aircraft was made available to respond to requests from other government departments, including the Coastguard and HM Customs.

The RAF component was reinforced by the arrival of 230 Squadron, with its Westland Puma HC1 medium support helicopters. Its task was to provide the full range of assistance to the police and army day and night, seven days a week, 52 weeks of the year. The aircraft is perfect for

A Westland Aerospatiale Puma of 230 Squadron flying above the Ulster countryside.
J Woods

The Chinook airlift to Langford Lodge.   *J Woods*

Northern Ireland duties, being fairly fast and capacious and has been described as an 'airborne four-ton truck'.

A much larger helicopter, a Chinook of 7 Squadron, was involved in a spectacular lifting operation on behalf of the Ulster Aviation Society, when, on 7 April, ZD574 ferried a rather difficult underslung load. The second pre-production prototype Short SD-330 G-BDBS (generously donated and repainted by the company) was transported from Nutts Corner to Langford Lodge to occupy a place of honour in the Society's museum collection.

More New Works

In June 1993 the 108 bedroom Novotel Belfast International Hotel was opened to the public. It also provided a restaurant and bar, conference and banqueting suite, as well as a fitness room and sauna. Being situated some 60 metres from the main terminal entrance, it could hardly have been more convenient. To complement this construction, the exit and entrance hall was much improved and a canopy was provided over the set down and pick-up areas, considerably enhancing the overall first impression on arriving at the airport. Inside the terminal, the catering and retail outlets were overhauled, as was the check-in hall.

Also in June, American Trans Air replaced its charter-only service to New York, with the addition of provision for scheduled passengers. Sadly, in 1993 Ulster Maple Leaf Travel came to an end, closing a chapter in the air transport history of the province. During nearly 30 years of operations it is estimated that the company flew nearly 100,000 Ulster people safely to their holiday destinations.

To Dublin by DC-8

By the 1990s the elegant DC-8 was becoming increasingly rare. Three examples were operated by the Irish airline Translift on a summer charter service from Belfast to Orlando, for Air Canada Vacations and Falcon Holidays. After arriving in Belfast, the aircraft had to position to Dublin empty. For sharp eyed members of the Ulster Aviation Society this was too good an opportunity to miss. An arrangement was made whereby on 5 September 44 members flew to Dublin on EI-TLD, a DC-8-71, for a nominal charge. The flight took only 15 minutes, but was a memorable experience for all on board.

A DC-8 of the Irish airline Translift, which provided a short but enjoyable flight from Belfast to Dublin for members of the Ulster Aviation Society.   *J Woods*

Further Bad News

Unfortunately, British Midland withdrew two services during the year – firstly the Paris route in January and then, in October, the East Midlands schedule was transferred to sister airline Manx Airways at the City Airport. The final service was undertaken by a Manx ATP, G-PEEL at the end of the month. The Gill Air service to Newcastle and the Brymon European to Humberside also stopped, the last flight being by the Jetstream 31 G-OBEA on 31 October.

This year may well be seen as the lowest point in the airport's fortunes – particularly with respect to scheduled services, with only the following being provided: British Airways to Heathrow, Manchester and Glasgow; British Midland to Heathrow and Jersey (seasonal only); Maersk Air (which had bought Birmingham European when it de-merged from Brymon) to Birmingham; Air UK to Leeds/Bradford; Britannia to Luton; and KLM to Amsterdam.

Worse news was to follow in January 1994 when Britannia pulled out, the final schedule being flown by 737-200 G-BHWE on 9 January. The connection had proved popular, but Britannia was retiring its Boeing 737 fleet in order to standardise on 757s and 767s, which were too big to be economically viable on a useful but not essential route. Air UK added to the woe by transferring the Leeds/Bradford schedule to the City Airport in the spring.

The only comfort came from the Heathrow trunk route (which was generating over 50% of the airport's total passengers, while maintaining its position as one of the UK's busiest domestic schedules), the continuing success of the cargo operations and the charter traffic to the ever popular Florida, Canada and the Mediterranean. None of these services could feasibly be moved from Aldergrove. The competition from the City Airport was hurting Belfast International badly, but it could not take over routes which required large aircraft as its runway was not long enough, nor could it provide the round the clock opening hours essential for freight and holiday flights.

Privatisation

It was against this rather gloomy background that in February parliament passed the Airports (Northern Ireland) Order 1994, which enabled the airport to be privatised by way of a trade sale. On the credit side it was a business that could hardly fail, as an international airport is an essential part of any country's infrastructure. There had been considerable investment of government and European cash to enhance and modernise the facilities, while the long-term growth potential of commercial aviation is vast. On 20 July 1994 a management buy-out for the sum of £32.75 million resulted in the creation of Belfast International Airport Holdings Ltd, with Jim Dornan continuing as managing director, a post he had held since the previous year.

The search for new business was to be an immediate priority, with the continuation of a more dynamic marketing policy, approaching targeted airlines to initiate new routes and attract new operators. Three new airlines started services during the year – Knight Air using Bandeirantes to Leeds/Bradford on 31 October; Genesis, with the appropriately registered Jetstream 31 G-ENIS to East Midlands on 31 November; and Emerald European BAC 1-11s to Luton on 15 December. None, however, was successful, with only Knight Air lasting more than a few months.

Knight Air used Embraer Bandeirantes on its Leeds/Bradford route.

S Boyd

The final Emerald European flight to Belfast approaching runway 25 on 8 August 1995.
G Adams

British Airways had been continuing to re-structure its services, with Maersk operating to Birmingham "in BA livery and with a style of onboard service consistent with British Airways".[77] From July the Glasgow flights were taken over by Loganair acting as a BA franchise – BA Express.

The Buccaneer

On 4 April 1994 a Royal Air Force HS Buccaneer S2B travelled to RAF Aldergrove from RAF Lossiemouth – not in itself that remarkable an event, but this example was special as it had been bought by the Ulster Aviation Society. The original plan was to lift the aircraft by Chinook to its new resting place at Langford Lodge. However, this proved impractical owing to the weight of this very solidly built low-level strike aircraft, which had gained fame late in its 30 year career, with an impressive performance in the Gulf War. Removal by road was then considered, but the implications for trees and telegraph poles rendered this scheme unworkable also.

With considerable help from the Senior RAF Officer Northern Ireland and British Airways, who provided transport for the engineering team from Inverness, it was decided to fly the aircraft to Langford. As the aircraft was by then retired, it was fortunate that the last two remaining aircrew, Squadron Leader Martin Hopkins and Flight Lieutenant John Parsons, were also available. On the morning of 18 April the final flight in RAF service of the Buccaneer took place from Aldergrove to Langford, thereby also establishing (it is believed) the record for the shortest flight by the type – lasting one minute and 32 seconds.

The Chinook

A few weeks later, on 2 June, ZD576, a Chinook HC2 left Aldergrove carrying many of the province's senior security personnel to a conference in Scotland. In circumstances that have never been fully understood, it crashed on a hillside at Beinn na Lice on the Mull of Kintyre, with the loss of all on board. The Church of Ireland Primate, Archbishop Robin Eames, spoke movingly at the memorial service in St Anne's Cathedral: "It was the tragedy of the Troubles that took 29 lives. The nature of their passing and the tragic irony of that accident cannot remove the fact that their names and the names of all those who have given their lives in the service of law and order in Northern Ireland must not be forgotten. That total sacrifice, that total loss is as much a part of the search for peace as any other."[78]

72 Squadron

In September, 72 Squadron had a double celebration to mark 30 years of flying the Wessex and 25 years of duty in Northern Ireland. The commemorations began with the squadron colours being paraded before the Secretary of State, Sir Patrick Mayhew, while three Wessex flew past

Supermarine Spitfire P7350 *Enniskillen* in 72 Squadron markings and Westland Wessex over Co Antrim.   *J Woods*

with the RAF ensign in tow. The flying display which followed included the Red Arrows, the army Lynx team – the Blue Eagles and the Spitfire P7350 *Enniskillen*.

A Link Renewed and New Operators

When the British Midland ATP G-MAUD took off from East Midlands on the BD271 service to Belfast International on 16 January 1995, a connection which had lasted from 1965 to the take-over by Manx Airlines in October 1993 was reforged. More good news followed with two new carriers, Air Belfast (which was based at the airport) operating 1-11s to London Stansted and Business Air using 30-seat Saab 340 turboprops to Manchester.

This was followed on the charter front by the establishment of a dedicated check-in area on the elevated section of the departures concourse for two airlines which had gained a firm foothold in the market, Airtours and Air 2000. In July Aer Lingus, operating as Vacations Ireland, tested the transatlantic market with a summer charter service to Boston and New York via Shannon. The aircraft used was the latest widebody Airbus, the 331-passenger A330. A further new type was the Fokker 100, a development of the F28 Fellowship, which Deutsche BA

A BAe ATP of Manx Airlines.   *J Woods*

Local carrier Air Belfast used the BAC 1-11 on the London Stansted route.   *J Woods*

Top: Business Air provided a service to Manchester using the 30-seat Saab 340.

J Woods

Two names that would become very familiar to holidaymakers:

Middle: Airtours, with the Airbus A320.

J Woods

Bottom: Air 2000, with the Boeing 757.

S Boyd

Top: Aer Lingus, operating as Vacations Ireland, used the Airbus A330 on a summer charter service to Boston and New York, via Shannon.

J Woods

Middle: Deutsche BA employed the Fokker 100 on the Munich–Kerry–Belfast–Munich holiday route.

J Woods

Bottom: Jersey European provided competition with Air Belfast on the London Stansted route, here using the BAC 1-11.

J Woods

Robinson R22 and R44 of Helicopter Training and Hire, which had formerly been based at Newtownards.   *J Woods*

operated on a Munich–Kerry–Belfast–Munich holiday route. Finally, in November, Jersey European commenced a service to Stansted in competition with Air Belfast.

Civil Helicopter Operations

On the general aviation front Helicopter Training and Hire moved to the airport from its former base at Newtownards. Over the following months it was to develop considerably, with the construction of purpose built facilities to house the aircraft, providing maintenance, classroom and office accommodation. A full range of rotary-wing activity was being offered from training to commercial pilot standard, to corporate and personal, business or pleasure flying, as well as aerial filming and photography. The growing fleet started with the basic two-seat piston engine Robinson R22, to which were added the gas turbine powered Augusta-Bell JetRanger and the four-seat Robinson R44. HT & H were to be joined soon by

another helicopter operator, Eurojet, with another JetRanger.

Air Force One

Following the terrorist cease-fires, the US President and First Lady, Bill and Hillary Clinton, arrived in Northern Ireland on 30 November 1995 to add their weight to the peace process. Not only Air Force One VC-25A 29000 (an executive conversion of the Boeing 747) arrived at Aldergrove. It was accompanied by a considerable collection of other first time visitors to the province, bearing security staff, limousines, helicopters, the presidential entourage and a large media contingent. These included the back-up VC-25A, two C-137s (military 707s), three massive C-5 Galaxy transporters, the press corps 747 of Tower Air and four helicopters – two VH-60 Seahawks, one MH-53 Sea Dragon and a CH-53 Super Stallion. The sight and thunderous sound of the helicopter formations

Left and below: Air Force One, a Boeing VC-25A, arrives at Belfast International Airport with President and Mrs Clinton on 30 November 1995.

J Woods

crossing Belfast Lough and passing along the Glengormley Gap was a particular memory of an important few days.

Freight Business

In April 1995 the Ulster Aviation Society was invited to visit the cargo centre by the Servisair freight manager, John Emerson. The following is an extract from an article by the author which appeared in the Society's journal, the *Ulster Airmail*:

A long serving general cargo operator, Hunting Cargo Airlines, flies a rotation to Coventry every night. The 15 ton capacity Lockheed Electra has had to be replaced recently by the larger 18 ton capacity Vickers Merchantman, which also offers useful additional hold space. Hunting are confident that the Belfast business will continue to grow and intend to introduce the 24 ton capacity Boeing 727-200. Four of these aircraft are being purchased by the

group, all fully hushkitted to meet Stage 3 noise requirements.

On being asked the meaning of General Cargo, Hunting manager, Bob Stokes replied, "Anything from blood plasma to grass seeds, from crystal vases to live eels." High value, perishable or urgent low volume freight items are the staple diet. Another major freight company serving Northern Ireland is TNT. A Boeing 727-200 has replaced their BAe 146-300 QT and is based in Belfast on a nightly round trip to Cologne via Birmingham. So this classic trijet will soon be a familiar sight for local enthusiasts. A third regular general cargo operator is Channel Express, which uses a Handley Page Herald for flights to Liverpool.

Royal Mail operations form a vital part of the cargo system. Some 15 tons are carried each way across the Irish Sea every night. Seven aircraft fly to seven destinations, departing between 8pm and 11pm, returning between 1am and 3am. This contract is

Three examples of Belfast International's role as a freight handler:

Top: A TNT Boeing 727.
Belfast International Airport

Middle: A Channel Express Handley Page Herald.
J Woods

Bottom: An Emerald Airways Hawker Siddeley 748.
J Woods

much sought after and a very high level of efficiency and punctuality is demanded by the Post Office from the airlines involved. Sorting the mail is carried out onsite, in a facility within the cargo terminal, between 7pm and 3am.

Newspapers are flown in from Liverpool in Emerald Airways HS 748 Srs 2A G-ATMI, G-ATMJ, G-AYIM and G-BPDA. Normally three aircraft are used but it can be four on a busy night.

The Cargo Centre also deals with the loads brought in the holds of scheduled passenger services, though British Airways handles its own relatively low volume share of the business.

Short Belfasts and Boeing 707 freighters are relatively common sights. However in the last few months the Russians have started to come and it is confidently predicted by the Cargo Manager that more are on the way. Recent visitors have been the Ilyushin IL76 taking away a consignment of cigarettes to Alma Ata

and an Antonov AN124 bearing generators from FG Wilson to Haiti. This last occasion allowed two giant freighters, a Belfast and the Antonov to be photographed on the ramp together.

In January 1995 an IL76 was ordered in a hurry to take 15 tons of mushrooms to Stansted – the bad weather had meant that they could not go by sea and their shelf life was limited. Another unusual load was packed into a 707 in October 1994 – this time it was 15 tons of egg boxes for South Africa. A disastrous fire in Johannesburg had destroyed the local egg box factory.

On 26th April, a group from the society visited the Cargo Centre and spent an evening on the ramp watching the loading process, following which we witnessed the departure of a stream of aircraft and finally we were given a guided tour of the Royal Mail operation by the managers, Harry Donnelly and David Hoey. These proved to be a fascinating few hours, with the time passing all too quickly. Our host

Top: Short Belfast freighter.
Belfast International Airport

Bottom: The Russians are coming! From left to right, a Tupolev TU-134, an Ilyushin IL-76 and an Antonov AN124.
Belfast International Airport

Top: The Royal Mail used British World Airlines Vickers Viscounts for the carriage of parcels.

J Woods

Bottom: Woodgate Executive used Britten Norman Trislander for letters.

J Woods

allowed us close access to the aircraft, including inside the two Viscounts, one of which was carrying a consignment of local oysters. It was obvious from the efficient way in which the work was carried out, that John runs a tightly knit and happy operation. Indeed to keep fit and active, he often lends a hand with the loading himself. Highlights of the visit included the impressive take-off of the Merchantman and the rather longer run of the heavily laden 727 on runway 07.

The following aircraft were seen:

General Cargo

Hunting Cargo Airlines Vickers V.953C Merchantman G-APEP "Superb"- Coventry. TNT Express Boeing 727-281F EI-TNT – Birmingham-Cologne.

Channel Express HP Herald 210 G-SCTT – Liverpool.

Royal Mail Parcels

British World Airlines Vickers V.802 Viscount G-OPFE – Coventry.

British World Airlines Vickers V.836 Viscount G-BFZL – Coventry.

Royal Mail Letters

Titan Airways Shorts SD360 G-ZAPD – Gatwick and Stansted.

BAC Leasing EMB-110P1 Bandeirante G-DBAC – Gatwick and Stansted.

(These two aircraft were replacements for the usual HS748.)

Woodgate Executive BN-2A MkIII Trislander G-WEAC – Edinburgh. (Recently introduced by the company after an epic ferry flight from Africa.)

Business Air Saab SF.340A G-GNTA – East Midlands.

Gill Aviation Shorts SD330 G-BIOE – Bristol.

Gill Aviation Shorts SD360 G-DASI – Liverpool.[79]

Top: British Regional, operating as British Airways Express, served the Manchester route using BAe 146s.

J Woods

Middle: A Fokker 100 of Air UK, used on the Amsterdam schedule which was taken over from KLM.

J Woods

Bottom: Community Express, using the BAe Jetstream 31, offered a service to Liverpool.

Belfast International Airport

More Arrivals and Departures

The early months of 1996 saw the ending of Air Belfast, Business Air (which was purchased by the Airlines of Britain Group) and Knight Air schedules. British Airways also transferred the Manchester service to British Regional (formerly Manx Airlines (Europe) and also part of the Airlines of Britain), which was to operate as a franchisee under the BA Express label, using BAe 146s. This left Heathrow as the only route flown directly by the national carrier. In July Air UK took over the Amsterdam schedule from KLM. Meanwhile, Aer Lingus had extended their transatlantic service to a year round basis and were now providing a full scheduled operation. In the autumn, for a brief period, Community Express offered a service to Liverpool before the company folded.

A more unusual arrival was the British World Viscount G-OPFE on 29 March, which landed on runway 07 with the undercarriage raised. It was lifted by slings and cranes a few hours later and the wheels were deployed to enable the aircraft to be parked out of the way. The blades of all four propellers were bent back like banana skins and the bright red Parcel Force livery was scraped to the bare metal under the fuselage. It was later declared to be beyond economic repair and was broken up – with the crew seats being kindly donated to the Ulster Aviation Society clubroom.

During the year a very welcome cargo schedule was maintained for a time by a Heavylift Short Belfast to Manchester and Amsterdam. The summer IT programme showed a marked increase in services to the USA and Canada, with Air Transat, Air Club, Royal, Airtours, Britannia, Leisure International, World Airways and American Trans Air providing flights, using Tristars, 747s, 767s, DC-10s and a newcomer, the MD-11 – a widebody tri-jet derived from the DC-10. The growing Florida market added another destination to the well-established

(Continued on page 116)

Two of the carriers to Canada and the USA:

Top: An Air Transat Lockheed L-1011.
S Boyd

Bottom: An Air Club Boeing 747.
Belfast International Airport

Three further examples of carriers on the transatlantic route:

Top: A Royal Airbus 310-300.
S Boyd

Middle: An Airtours Boeing 767.
J Woods

Bottom: A World Airways McDonnell Douglas MD-11.
Belfast International Airport

The summer of 1996 saw regular visits by the likes of:

Top: American Trans Air Boeing 757s.

J Woods

Middle: Air Europa 757s.

J Woods

Bottom: Spanair McDonnell Douglas MD-83s.

J Woods

Airtours and Balkan were two important providers of charter services in the mid-1990s.

Top: An Airbus A320 of Airtours.

J Woods

Bottom: A Tupolev TU-154 of Balkan.

M Steenson

(Continued from page 113)

Orlando – the ex-Marine Corps base at Sanford. European carriers showed no great changes with Air Europa, Futura, Spanair, Airtours, Air 2000 and Balkan dominating.

A Revival of the Air Display

Display flying of a kind returned to the airport on 3 August. On this occasion the public was given the chance to inspect, on the ground, the wide range of aircraft that were parked at Aldergrove in preparation for the Ulster Air Show at Newtownards the following day. Pleasure flying also made a comeback in the shape of the elegant and refined 50 year old veteran DH89 Rapide of Air Caernarfon G-AIDL. An alternative was the Jet Ranger helicopter G-ISKY of Belfast International-based Eurojet, which was taking a break from its normal routine of morning radio roadwatch duties.

Farewell to an Old Favourite

On 30 September there occurred a very sad farewell, with the final departure by the last surviving Vickers Merchantman G-APEP *Superb*. In its earlier guise as a BEA

The end of an era – the last Vickers Merchantman to depart Aldergrove, G-APEP *Superb*.   *J Woods*

Vanguard it had been flying into Belfast since 1963 – a remarkable career. The first Vanguard schedule to Nutts Corner had been two years earlier. At their zenith Vanguards had operated over 50 return flights to London a week (at a standby off-peak rate of £6 single in 1970). In the late 1960s they were converted to freighters for BEA, and from 1979 the type was operated by Air Bridge Carriers, subsequently Hunting Cargo Airlines. In the course of researching this book, and in the writing of other articles, the author has heard nothing but praise for this aeroplane from aircrew, engineers, airline staff, baggage handlers and enthusiasts alike.

Chapter 10

TBI *and the Future*

The Coming of TBI

TBI became the new owners of the airport on 13 August 1996. The editor of the *Ulster Airmail* greeted the announcement with cautious optimism:

> The news that Belfast International Airport has been bought in a £107m deal by the property and leisure group TBI, owners of Cardiff Airport, has generated much comment on the government's £33m valuation two years ago and envy of the good fortune/foresight of those able to take part in the management buy-out who now see their investment being returned more than a hundred fold. TBI have done well with Cardiff, by all accounts, but the two airports are very different in the nature of the competition they face and the investment they need. However, we welcome the confidence shown by the new owners in the airport and its staff and hope that their aim of attracting other aviation related businesses to Aldergrove can be achieved.[80]

TBI's own thoughts on the matter can be judged from the chief executive, Keith Brooks, writing in the 1996 Annual Report:

> Airports provide TBI with a tremendous opportunity to take advantage of its entrepreneurial approach and tough business and cash disciplines. Airports are fundamentally simple businesses and the main economic drivers are passengers numbers and passenger spend supplemented by freight and property opportunities. More passengers means increased income from the airlines but more passengers will only be attracted if the choice of destinations is right and the facilities are fully up to the standards expected of a modern airport.[81]

The long transition from being what was effectively a public utility to becoming a wholly business oriented enterprise was nearly at hand. However, TBI impressed by not rushing to make major changes without careful assessment. Part of the company's culture is to listen and learn as well as to be positive and energetic.

Taking Stock

The year 1997 was a relatively quiet on the surface, with few dramatic developments. Jersey European began the year by moving the entire Stansted operation from the City

A Jersey European BAC 1-11 – the airline moved its Stansted operation to Belfast International in early 1997.   *J Woods*

Airport, which lessened the confusion that a split service caused in the minds of passengers. A BAC 1-11, G-AVMK was leased from European Aviation and painted in JEA livery to fly the route. In May, TBI added to its airport collection with the purchase of Sanford in Florida, a shrewd buy considering that the southern state is the most popular holiday destination in the world. The summer IT programme followed the well-established pattern, with one new destination, the Dominican Republic.

Despite the cancellation of the Newtownards section of the Ulster Air Weekend in June, a large collection of static aircraft was again on view at Aldergrove, with pleasure flights this time being provided in a Scottish Aviation Twin Pioneer G-APRS, owned by Air Atlantique. The following extract from the *Ulster Airmail* describes a flight in the aircraft:

> ... the arrival had been impressive enough but that was nothing compared to the roar and clatter of the twin radials bursting into noisy life – this was no "gentleman's aerial carriage" like last year's marvellous DH Rapide – but rather, a no-nonsense working aircraft, built like coal lorry. However, as our pilot, Paul Freestone, said, she was very pleasant to fly – handling in some respects better than a DC-3. We spent a thoroughly happy 35 minutes growling over the environs of Lough Neagh at 1500 feet and some 95kts. Our first gentle approach to land was aborted and we received a very good impression of the power reserves available and the low speed lift as we swiftly climbed away at full throttle. I could well imagine that if you were stuck in a jungle clearing then the sight and sound of the solid, reliable Twin Pin would be immensely reassuring.[82]

A New Managing Director

The man with responsibility for taking stock, arrived at the airport in the summer of 1997. Paul Kehoe had been appointed as TBI's new managing director. It was interesting to note that instead of bringing in merely a company man or 'bean counter', the new MD had an aviation background – evidence of TBI's strategy being based on common sense rather than on doctrine.

Paul quickly became a friend of the Ulster Aviation Society, as the *Airmail* report of his visit to the monthly meeting in January 1998 showed:

> We had the pleasure of welcoming Paul Kehoe, the MD of Belfast International Airport. Paul has been in the job for six months and admitted that the time had flown by very quickly since his appointment.

With the aid of some very impressive high-tech projection equipment, he gave the meeting an extensive overview of the plans being made to develop the airport. These he divided into five main areas: increased passenger air traffic, enhanced terminal catering and shopping facilities, improved check-in and passenger handling, growth of the cargo market and greater use of the site for business development.

The prospect of services by a "low-cost" carrier such as easyJet or Ryanair was raised, as was the prospect of direct services to more European destinations. Paul said that really significant growth relied on two main factors: the achievement of a political settlement leading to greater inward tourist travel and the concentration of all civil traffic at Belfast International. By these means he believed that what he termed the "critical mass" of 5 million passengers per annum could be reached.

He also felt that it was important to change the working culture of the airport, encouraging much more sideways communication between departments rather than up and down the management chain, thus giving greater individual responsibility. Moreover, he added, the travelling and visiting public had a right to enjoy the experience of visiting the airport and that all staff should be working together to achieve this aim. Paul's style of management was, he said, an "open" one and proof of this may indeed be found in his willingness to address the Society in such a frank and honest way.[83]

New Services, New Airlines, Links Re-newed, Farewell to an Old Friend

The end of an era is indeed a hackneyed phrase but is fully justifiable in the case of the final departures of the British World Vickers Viscounts G-AOHM and G-OPFI, resplendent in their red Parcel Force livery, on 8 January.

A BAe Jetstream 41 of BA Express, used on the new Edinburgh service.   *J Woods*

Top: British Midland introduced the Airbus A321 on the Heathrow route.

J Woods

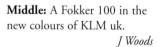

Middle: A Fokker 100 in the new colours of KLM uk.

J Woods

Bottom: Sabena inaugurated a service to Brussels, using a BAe 146.

J Woods

Top: A Bombardier CRJ-200 was introduced on the Birmingham route by Maersk Air, in BA livery.

J Woods

Middle: An An-124 is used to transport the first CRJ-700 fuselage (manufactured by Shorts) from Belfast to Montreal.

J Woods

Bottom: The first easyJet to arrive at Belfast International was a Boeing 737 G-EZYG on 18 September 1997.

J Woods

A touch of nostalgia was provided by this Lockheed Constellation which night-stopped at Belfast International. It was in Northern Ireland for displays at Enniskillen, St Angelo and Newtownards.

J Woods

Another link with the first day of operations in 1963 was gone. Now only the cargo-carrying Fokker F27 and the occasional ad-hoc DC-3 survived as types that had visited the terminal on day one, 35 years before.

The first of a surge of new developments began on 1 March 1998, with the restoration of an Edinburgh schedule by British Regional (operating as BA Express), using Jetstream 41s. Later in the year the airline also transferred its Aberdeen and Cardiff services from the City Airport. On 6 April British Midland introduced their brand new 195-seat Airbus A321, G-MIDA, onto the Heathrow route. In May Fokker 100, G-UKFC, arrived in the new KLM uk colours, following the absorption of the British airline by the Dutch flag carrier, while Airtours introduced a leased Boeing 747 on the Orlando–Sanford charter service.

A major event in June was the establishment of a direct scheduled service to Brussels by Sabena, with the first fight being flown on 2 June by BAe RJ-100, OO-DWD (a modernised version of the BAe 146). Later in the same month, on the Birmingham route, Maersk Air (in BA livery) introduced the Bombardier CRJ-200 (CRJ) G-MSKK. Six of these 50-passenger 'regional jets' had been ordered by the airline to replace the vintage BAC 1-11s. They are particularly significant for Belfast as the centre fuselage section, wing-mounted flight control surfaces and engine nacelles are all manufactured by Shorts which has, since 1989, been part of the Canadian aerospace group, Bombardier. Indeed, on 28 September, the first fuselage for the larger CRJ-700 was shipped from Aldergrove to Montreal in an An-124 of Heavylift. The CRJ and its Brazilian rival, the Embraer RJ series may prove important types for the airport over the next decade, perhaps opening

up more direct business travel oriented routes to European cities.

Equally meaningful for the potential growth of traffic was the arrival of easyJet and its low-cost operation to London Luton, on 18 September, flown by the 737 G-EZYG. The airline was founded in 1995 by Stelios Haji-Ioannou. Its approach is radically different to that of most other airlines and is geared to the low cost strategy. Direct booking to the airline by telephone or the Internet cuts out the travel agent. There is no ticket, but merely a letter of confirmation and a reference number to be presented at the check-in. Seats are not allocated, but those who check in earliest board first and so have first choice. Food on-board is sold rather than handed out. The aircraft themselves, Boeing 737-300s, are brightly painted, with the booking telephone number prominent. The airline has expanded rapidly to offer a range of destinations in the UK and Europe.

A nostalgic visitor at the end of June was the Lockheed L-749 Constellation N494TW, which night-stopped at the airport when displaying at Newtownards and Enniskillen, St Angelo. More American hardware had landed earlier in the month, with the brief return of Mr and Mrs Clinton, though oddly this visit aroused less interest among enthusiasts than previously. The only downbeat note in a year of sustained progress was the withdrawal of Jersey European's Stansted service back to Belfast City.

230 Squadron

While celebrating its 80th anniversary in 1998, this Aldergrove based squadron was also involved in the most

Among the military helicopters operating out of RAF Aldergrove in the late 1990s were the following:

Top: A Wessex and a Puma of 72 and 230 Squadrons.
RAF Aldergrove

Middle: The Westland Lynx of 655 Squadron AAC.
J Woods

Bottom: The Westland Aerospatiale Gazelle of 665 Squadron AAC.

J Woods

A Westland Sea King of 846
Naval Air Squadron.

J Woods

tragic event of the year, the aftermath of the Omagh bombing. Crews from the squadron answered the call for medical evacuation and the Pumas operated for many hours, ferrying the injured to hospitals in Belfast. Later, the commanding officer said: "It was a very harrowing day. The crews coped extremely well. I was very proud of them all."[84]

At the end of the year, as well as the Wessex HC2 and Puma HC1 helicopters of 72 and 230 Squadrons, military aircraft based at Aldergrove included those on the strength of 5 Regiment, Army Air Corps. These were the Lynx AH7s of 655 Squadron, Gazelle AH1s of 665 Squadron and the Islander AL1s of 1 Flight. Two units also detached aircraft for service in Northern Ireland, 7 Squadron with Chinook HC2s and the Sea King HC4s of 846 Naval Air Squadron – though the naval element departed in March 1999, having been at Aldergrove for five years.

More Building

The expansion of the freight business resulted in the need for the construction of a new cargo agents' warehouse, which came into use in July, while on 12 November the Duke of Edinburgh opened the new £6 million kerbside check-in hall. This airy and spacious construction, which allowed passengers henceforth to deposit their baggage before proceeding into the main terminal building, saw the stilling of one very familiar voice, the automated "You are now approaching the end of the moving walkway. Please remember to push your trolley over the ramp," which had accompanied millions of journeys over the years. The old check-in desks and baggage conveyor equipment were sent to TBI's latest acquisition, Stockholm's Skavsta Airport.

Another departure was that of the 35 year-old Handley Page Herald G-EBYF of Channel Express, operating for Emerald Airways, on 26 March 1999 – marking the final appearance of the last of this type at the airport.

Towards the Twenty-first Century

Aldergrove has been in existence for more than three-quarters of the twentieth century. Aircraft first flew from the site only 15 years after the era of powered, heavier-than-air flight began. It has been adapted and altered over the years to meet the changing requirements and circumstances of the time. Sometimes the view taken was rather short-term. At others, social and economic considerations were a major influence and indeed, a hindrance to coherent sustained growth. Today's fast-changing world often simply does not allow the opportunity to take a long view and so make flexible and sensible plans for the future.

It is therefore greatly to his credit that Paul Kehoe, after 18 months in position as managing director of Belfast International has, resulting from much careful thought and discussion, developed a strategic master-plan to take the airport into the twenty-first century. To begin with, it was important to highlight the tasks that he had been set by the Board of TBI. These were to increase revenue, to control costs and to raise the profile of the airport, thus laying the foundations of future growth. He then had to identify the strengths and weaknesses of the airport in relation to those goals.

The committed, enthusiastic and operationally focused staff were an important asset, to which have been added the infusion of a new, more open management culture and the

Among the wide variety of aircraft in BA livery using Belfast International in 1999 were these two:

Top: The Canadair Dash 8.

J Woods

Bottom: The Embraer ERJ-145, used on the Cardiff service.

J Woods

recruitment of a few key personnel with specific skills.

The reliance on one main route, London Heathrow, was a marked weakness. This problem has been addressed and, as has been noted above, several old links have been renewed and new services started. To these were added, during the course of 1999, the extension of the Maersk (BA franchise) operation through Birmingham to Vienna and Geneva; the re-introduction of a Newcastle connection, provided by BA subsidiary Brymon Airways (the inaugural service being flown by DHC-8-300 G-BRYY on 2 May, though a year later the service transferred to Belfast City), with some flights going on to Copenhagen; the addition of a new easyJet service to Liverpool (on 15 July, flown by the Boeing 737-300, G-EZYJ); and the return of Gill Airways passenger services to Newcastle and Teeside (if only for a

few months). British Midland and British Regional began operating the 50-seat Embraer ERJ-145 to the airport from East Midlands and Cardiff respectively.

On the debit side, in a surprising move, KLM uk withdrew from the Amsterdam route at the end of October, the last service being operated by the Fokker 100, G-UKFO, on Sunday 30 October. Every effort is being made to add further destinations, with Paris, a major German city, Newark in the USA and Toronto being particularly desirable.

The charter and holiday market was already quite strong, but too many passengers are still choosing Dublin, so the aim in this area is to offer the greatest degree of choice possible and so encourage travellers to fly from Belfast. Inbound tourism cannot realistically be expanded to any greater extent without political stability and the absence of civil disturbance, factors which are, of course, outside the airport marketing staff's control, much as they are to be desired.

By the end of 1999, a new record yearly passenger figure in excess of three million had been achieved for the first time. During the course of the year 2000 several services were expanded and a new one added. In May, however, the Brymon connection moved to Belfast City. British Airways introduced a new type on the London Heathrow route on 3 June – the A319, G-EUPJ, being the first of the latest and smallest member of the Airbus family to arrive at the airport. The major developments at the International Airport came in the autumn. EasyJet announced an increase in its schedules to Luton, now five flights each weekday; and Liverpool, which increased to four flights each weekday from October and then to six in December. There was also the announcement of an easyJet direct connection to Amsterdam, beginning in 2001 with a single daily rotation. Another 'low-cost' airline, GO, began a three-times daily service to London Stansted on 1

November with the arrival of the Boeing 737-300 G-IGOR. Sabena also increased its Brussels connection to three flights, six days a week. Aer Lingus also planned to add to its transatlantic schedule via Shannon.

All in all, in November it was possible to predict another record year in total passenger numbers, international passengers and cargo tonnage. The stengthening economy was boosting air freight considerably, with Airbus A300 cargo aircraft becoming increasingly frequent visitors.

Looking to the future, the aim is not for the airport to become a 'hub' (ie focal point for connecting services), except in a very localised sense. The most obvious example of a hub in the UK is Heathrow, followed by Gatwick and Manchester. In northern Europe the major hubs are Paris, Frankfurt, Amsterdam, Brussels and Copenhagen. At all of these the greatest problem is congestion and the lack of available 'slot times' (ie arrival and departure times). Belfast International will fit into this pattern as a major spoke to a number of hubs, offering alternatives to more crowded airports, which is one reason why broadening the list of UK and European destinations offered is so important. In order

Above: A view of the General Aviation apron.

J Woods

to increase traffic, conveniently timed and frequent flights are essential, which is more achievable at secondary hubs. The low-cost carriers such as easyJet, Ryanair, GO and Virgin Express are important in offering alternative hubs, such as those being developed at Luton, Stansted and Liverpool.

An airport does not just need aircraft and destinations. The infrastructure and passengers facilities have to be of the highest quality.

TBI are prepared to fund badly needed additional road and rail links, a second terminal, and to develop the Genesis Business Park on 190 acres surrounding the airport – if it makes sound business sense to make this considerable investment. The plans are flexible and can be adapted to meet the level of growth, should it exceed or fail to reach anticipated levels. A good example of this is Terminal 2, which would be located to the east side of the present terminal. Planning permission has been granted; it can be constructed in its entirety or a new pier could be built, or simply extra ramp space could be created. As a whole, Terminal 2 would be a highly significant project, costing in the region of £13 million, with the capacity for two million passengers, 21 check-in desks and eight aircraft stands, four of which would be accessed by airbridges.

Freight traffic now depends considerably on the number of passengers carried, as a large proportion of cargo can be taken in the belly holds of airliners. But, if the Genesis Business Park develops strongly, then it is likely to benefit the cargo market. TBI has indicated that it is prepared to put up to £100 million into this project, which would involve call centres, office buildings, serviced offices, warehousing and a factory outlet centre. It has been estimated that Genesis could generate up to 15,000 jobs in Northern Ireland over a ten year period. It is also a possibility, again as a result of the continued overcrowding of European skies, that a specialised freight hub could be set up in Belfast. One advantage is that the airport is environmentally friendly with regard to population centres in the immediate vicinity, which could also lend itself to aircraft servicing or crew training work.

General Aviation will also continue to occupy an important niche. The current level of business is healthy but low-key. Mike Woodgate's company, which was split up, has now come together again under the ownership of Allan Keen and provides general charter, air-taxi, air ambulance and flying training services, as well as sales, maintenance and servicing. The largest GA aircraft based at the airport are the BN Trislanders, but a move to turbine power is the inevitable next step, probably in the shape of a Short 330/360 and a Beechcraft King Air. Locally based flying training and ad-hoc charter flying will continue to produce Ulster-born airline captains to add to those now flying with many of the major companies. There is no doubt that whatever the future holds, the management and staff, of what is now considerably more than 170 acres near Crumlin, will continue their vital work, which has made such a massive contribution to the social and economic well-being of the country, since a young flyer first visited the spot over 80 years ago.

Operational Facilities

Runways, Aprons, Hangars and Stands

The airport has two runways laid out so as to permit operations to be maintained under adverse crosswinds. The main runway, aligned on a compass bearing of 250/070 degrees is 2,777 metres long by 45 metres wide. It has a parallel taxiway and is of adequate length to permit the operation of all types and sizes of aircraft. The secondary, cross wind, runway, aligned on a compass bearing of 350/170 degrees is 1,951 metres long by 45 metres wide. The key advantages afforded by a cross wind runway, which is offered by few UK airports, are that it can operate in all weather conditions and that maintenance on the main runway is facilitated. Both runways have cambered friction course surfaces, together with 12.5 metres of hard shoulder.

The airfield has modern approach, runway and taxiway lighting with Precision Approach Path Indicators on all runways.

Apron areas total some 13.35 hectares of pavement.

There are two maintenance hangars at the western end of the airfield, one of which has the capacity to take aircraft up to the size of a Boeing 737.

The airport has 30 aircraft stands, three of which allow passenger access from the terminal to the aircraft, two being fitted with rotatable airbridges, while one has a fixed nose loader.

Control Tower, ATC and Landing Systems

The ATC facility at Belfast International, run by the Civil Aviation Authority, services the airport, military traffic for the adjoining MOD base, approach and departure cover for Belfast City Airport and en route traffic. It offers surveillance radar approaches on all runways. Subject to some limitations, approaches can also be made using the Doppler VHF Omni Range and distance measuring equipment (VOR/DME). The airfield is also equipped with a non-directional beacon (NDB) and direction finding apparatus.

The main runway is equipped with an Instrument Landing System (ILS) suitable for use down to visibility of Category IIIB weather conditions (the most severe grading equivalent to thick fog), while the secondary runway is equipped with an ILS for Category I conditions.

Secondary Surveillance Radar (SSR) became operational in the spring of 2000. It will give air traffic controllers greatly improved coverage of local movements, enabling them to see aircraft further out and at lower levels than was possible previously. Instead of only a blip on the screen, SSR accompanies the blip with the aircraft call sign, its ground speed and flying level. This makes the aircraft considerably easier to identify and reduces the requirement for so much coordination when passing movements between air traffic centres (eg Belfast to Scotland).

Appendix 2

Airlines, Routes and Aircraft

Key

S – Scheduled
C – Charter
F – Freight

Note

Airlines appear in chronological order of first becoming operative.

de Havilland Aeroplane Hire Service, 1922–23 (C, F)
Chester, Plymouth, Birmingham, Manchester, Dublin; DH16, DH50

Northern Airlines, 1924–25 (S)
Liverpool, Stranraer, Glasgow, Carlisle, Londonderry (diversions from Malone); DH9, DH50

Midland and Scottish Air Ferries, 1933–34 (S)
Glasgow, Campbeltown, Liverpool, Isle of Man, Romford; DH84, Avro 618/Ten, Avro 642, Airspeed Ferry

Hillman's Airways, 1934 (S)
Liverpool, Stapleford; DH84

Railway Air Services, 1934–36 (S, F)
London, Birmingham, Manchester, Glasgow, Isle of Man, Liverpool ; DH84, DH86, DH89, Westland Wessex

BEA, 1963–73; **BOAC**, 1968–71; **British Airways**, 1974– (S, C, F)
London Heathrow, Manchester, Birmingham, Glasgow, Jersey, Prestwick, New York, Newcastle, Leeds/Bradford, Liverpool, Isle of Man, Edinburgh, Bristol, Cardiff; HP Herald, Vickers Viscount, Vickers Vanguard, DH Comet, HS Trident, BAC 1-11, AW Argosy, Vickers Merchantman, Vickers VC-10, Boeing 707, Lockheed Tristar, Hawker Siddeley 748, Boeing 737, Boeing 757, Boeing 747, BAe Concorde, Boeing 767, BAe ATP, Airbus A320, Airbus A319

BKS Air Transport, 1963– ; **Northeast Airlines**, 1971–73 (S, F)
Newcastle, Dublin, Edinburgh, Leeds/Bradford, Teeside, Liverpool; DC-3, Airspeed Ambassador, Vickers Viscount, Bristol Britannia

Cambrian Airways, 1963–73 (S, F)
Liverpool, Isle of Man, Cardiff, Bristol, Prestwick, Edinburgh; Vickers Viscount, BAC 1-11

Derby AW, 1963– ; **British Midland AW**, 1964– ; **BM**, 1985– (S, C, F)
Derby, Carlisle, Enniskillen, Luton, East Midlands, Jersey, Toronto, Liverpool, Isle of Man, London Gatwick, London Heathrow, Paris, many European holiday destinations; DC-3, HP Herald, Canadair Argonaut, Vickers Viscount, BAC 1-11, Boeing 707, Fokker F 27, Short 330, Short 360, DC-9, BAe ATP, Boeing 737, Saab SF 340, Airbus A321, Fokker 70, Fokker 100, Embraer RJ-145, Airbus A320

British United (CI), **BU (Manx)**, 1963– ; **BUIA**, 1968– ; **BIA**, 1970– ; **Air UK**, 1980–93, 1996–98; **KLM uk**, 1998–99 (S, F)
Blackpool, Exeter, Bournemouth, Southampton, Isle of Man, Prestwick, Leeds/Bradford, Jersey, Amsterdam; DC-3, Herald, Viscount, Embraer Bandeirante, Short 330, Short 360, Fokker F 27, BAe 146, Fokker 100

British Eagle, 1963–66 (S)
London Heathrow; Bristol Britannia, Vickers Viscount

Aer Lingus, 1963– (S, C)
Dublin, Shannon, New York, Boston, Lourdes; Fokker F 27, Aviation Traders Carvair, Vickers Viscount, Boeing 707, BAC 1-11, Boeing 737, Boeing 747, Saab 340B, Airbus A 330, Lockheed Tristar, McDD MD11

Emerald Airways, 1965–67 (S, C, F)
Shannon, Prestwick, Londonderry, Enniskillen; DH Heron, Short Skyvan, DC-3

British United, 1966– ; **Caledonian/BUA**, 1970– ; **British Caledonian**, 1972–74 (S)
London Gatwick; BAC 1-11

Air Ulster, 1968–70 (S, C, F)
Prestwick; DC-3, Vickers Viscount

Autair, 1968 (S)
Teeside, Hull; HP Herald

Loganair, 1979–83, 1994–97 (as **BA Express**) (S, F)
Prestwick, Edinburgh, Glasgow; DH Twin Otter, BN Islander, BN Trislander, Fokker F 27, Short 330, Short 360

Dan Air, 1980–92 (S)
Newcastle, Cardiff, Bristol, Scatsta, London Gatwick, Teeside; HS 748, BAC 1-11, Boeing 727, BAe 146

NLM, 1980– ; **KLM**, 1983–96 (S)
Amsterdam; Fokker F 27, Fokker F 28, Saab 340B

Air Ecosse, 1980–86 (S, F)
Prestwick, Glasgow, Edinburgh, Dublin;
Embraer Bandeirante

Spacegrand, 1981–83 (S)
Blackpool;
Piper PA.31, Embraer Bandeirante, DH Twin Otter

Avair, 1982–83 (S)
Dublin; Beech King Air, Short 330

Genair, 1982–83 (S)
Teeside, Humberside; Short 330, Embraer Bandeirante

Manx Airlines, 1982–83; **British Regional Airlines** (as **BA Express**), 1996–(S)
Liverpool, Isle of Man, Manchester, Cardiff, Edinburgh, Aberdeen; Short 330, Fokker F 27, Embraer Bandeirante, BAe 146, BAe ATP, BAe Jetstream 41, Embraer RJ-145

Malinair, 1986–87 (S)
Aberdeen, Glasgow, Prestwick; BN Islander, Dornier 228

Iona National Airways, 1988 (S)
Dublin; Cessna Titan

TAT/Air France, 1988-90 (S)
Paris; Fokker F 28

Birmingham European AW, 1989– ; **Brymon European**, 1991– ; **Maersk Air**, 1993– (S)
Birmingham, Humberside;
Fokker 50, BAC 1-11, BAe Jetstream 31, DHC Dash 8, DHC Dash 7, Canadair CRJ-200, Boeing 737

Britannia Airways, 1989–94 (S)
London Luton; Boeing 737, Boeing 757, Boeing 767

Gill Air, 1991– ; **Gill Airways**, 1995– (S, F)
Newcastle, Teeside; Short 330, Short 360, ATR 72

Knight Air, 1994–96 (S)
Leeds/Bradford; Embraer Bandeirante

Genesis, 1994–95 (S)
East Midlands; BAe Jetstream 31

Emerald European, 1994–95 (S)
London Luton; BAC 1-11, Boeing 737 (on last service only)

Air Belfast, 1995–96 (S)
London Stansted, London Gatwick; BAC 1-11

Business Air, 1995–96 (S, F)
Manchester; Saab SF 340

Jersey European Airways, 1980, 1995–98 (C, S)
Jersey, London Stansted;
Vickers Viscount, BAC 1-11, BAe 146

Community Express, 1996 (S)
Liverpool; Short 360

Sabena, 1998– (S)
Brussels; BAe RJ-100, BAe 146

easyJet, 1998– (S)
London Luton, Liverpool, Amsterdam; Boeing 737

Brymon Airways, 1999–2000 (S)
Newcastle, Copenhagen; DHC Dash 8

GO, 2000– (S)
London Stansted; Boeing 737

Charter Operators:
Aeromaritime, Air Atlantis, Air Azores, Air Canada, Air Club, Air Europa, Air Europe, Air France, Air Jugoslavia, Air Liberte, Air Malta, Air National, Air Paris, Air Portugal, Air Spain, Air Sur, Air 2000, Air Toulouse, Airtours, Air Transat, Airworld, Air UK Leisure, All Leisure, American Trans Air, Austrian AL, Aviaco, Aviogenex, Balair, Balkan AL, BEA Airtours, Braathens, British Airtours, British Air Ferries, British World, Caledonian AW, Canada 3000, Canafrica, Capitol Airways, Cityjet/Virgin, CP Air, Corsair, Court Line, Croatian, Cyprus AW, Dan Air, Deutsche BA, Espania, Eurocypria, European Air Charter, Excalibur, Futura, Helios, Hispania, Iberia, Iberworld, Inexadria, International European, Istanbul AL, JMC Air, Laker AW, Lauda Air, Leisure International, Lineas Aereas Canarias, Lloyd International, Martinair, Monarch AW, Nationair, Norfly, Nortjet, Nouvelair, Nouvelaire Tunisie, Oasis, Olympic AW, Orion, Overseas National, Paramount, Pegasus, Quebecair, Rich International, Royal, Ryanair, Sabre AW, Saturn AW, Skyservice, Spanair, Spantax, Sterling, TEA, Transaer, Transavia, Transeuropa, Transglobe, Translift, Tarom, Tunis Air, Tyrolean, Viva, Wardair, World AW, Worldways Canada.

Charter Destinations:
Alicante, Almeria, Arrecife, Athens, Barcelona, Benghazi, Bergen, Berlin, Brussels, Bodrum, Boston, Budapest, Bucharest, Burgas, Calgary, Chambery, Cologne, Constantza, Corfu, Dalaman, Dubrovnik, Faro, Fuerteventura, Funchal, Geneva, Gerona, Grenoble, Halkidhiki, Heraklion, Ibiza, Innsbruck, Izmir, Jersey, Keflavik, Larnaca, Lamezia, Lanzarote, Las Palmas, Las Vegas, Linz, Lisbon, Ljubljana, Los Angeles, Lourdes, Lyon, Mahon, Malaga, Malta, Miami, Monastir, Montego Bay, Montreal, Munich, Nantes, Newark, New York, Orlando, Oslo, Palma, Paris, Paphos, Plovdiv, Porto, Prague, Puerta Plata, Pula, Puy, Reus, Rhodes, Riga, Rimini, Rome, Rotterdam, Rovaniemi, Salzburg, Salonica, Salou, Sanford, Santo Domingo, Split, Tenerife, Timisoara, Toronto, Toulouse, Treviso, Tunis, Turin, Vancouver, Varna, Vienna, Venice, Verona, Warsaw, Zakythnos, Zurich.

Charter Aircraft Types:
Airbus A300, A310, A320, A330; BAC 1-11, BAe Concorde, BAe 146; Boeing 707, 720, 727, 737, 747, 757, 767; Bristol Britannia; Canadair CL44; Convair CV440, CV580, CV990; DH Comet; Douglas DC-6, DC-7, DC-8, DC-9, DC-10; Fokker 70, 100; Ilyushin IL18; Lockheed Constellation, Tristar; McDD MD80, MD82, MD83, MD11; Saab 2000; Sud Aviation Caravelle; Tupolev TU134, TU154; Vickers Viscount; Yak 42.

Freight and Mail Services:
Aer Arann, Aer Turas, Air Atlantic, Air Atlantique, Air Bridge Carriers, Air Kilroe, Alidair, BAC Express, British Air Ferries, British Cargo AL, British World, Business Air, Capital AL, Channel Express, Comed, Dan Air, DHL, Elan, Emerald AW, Emery Worldwide, Evergreen International, Executive Air Charter, First Air, Flying Tiger, Gill Airways, Heavylift, Hunting Air Cargo, Invicta, Janes Aviation, Meenair, Mercury AW, Moscow Airlines, Polylot, Redcoat Air Cargo, Sagittair, Sayakhat, SAS, Securicor Air, Sky Guard, Southern, Streamline Aviation, Titan AW, Tradewinds AW, Transmeridian Air Cargo, TNT, United African, Vernair, Woodgate Aviation.

Freight Aircraft Types:
Airbus A300; ATL98 Carvair; AW Argosy; Antonov AN12, AN72, AN124; ATR 72, Avro York; Boeing 707, 727; BAe 146; Bristol Freighter, Britannia; BN Islander, Trislander; Canadair CL44; Cessna Titan; DH Heron; Douglas DC-3, DC-4, DC-6, DC-8; Fokker F27; HP Herald; HS 748; Ilyushin IL76; Lockheed Hercules, Lockheed Electra; Nord Noratlas; Piper Aztec, Chieftain; Saab SF 340; Short Belfast, Skyvan, 330, 360; Vickers Merchantman, Viscount.

The following types have also visited the airport for training or diversion: Airbus A340, Boeing 777, Ilyushin IL62 and IL86.

While every effort has been made to ensure that the above lists are exhaustive, some operators and types may have been inadvertently omitted. If so, the authors would be most grateful to have details of them.

Appendix 3

Aircraft used by the Three Principal Local Air Companies

Key

S –   Scheduled
C –   Charter
F –   Freight

A full listing of the aircraft used by three most significant air companies based at Aldergrove is as follows:

Emerald Airways, 1965–67 (S, C, F)
Short Skyvan G-ATPF, G-ATPG
(The first scheduled Skyvan service was flown by G-ATPF on 23 September 1966 from Londonderry to Glasgow.)
DH Heron: G-ALZL, G-AOZN, G-ARPK, G-ARUA, G-AROS
DC-3: EI-APB (ex G-AMWV), EI-APJ, EI-ARP, EI-ARR, G-AOGZ

Air Ulster, 1968–70 (S, C, F)
DC-3: G-AMJU, G-AMWV (registration restored), G-AGJV, G-ANAE, G-AMWW
Vickers Viscount EI-APD

Woodgate Aviation/Executive Air Charter, 1969– (C, F, air taxi, air ambulance, photography, flying training)
PA23 Aztec: G-ASFG, G-AWER, G-AZRG, G-ESKU (ex G-BCJS), G-CALL, G-ESKY (ex G-BBNN), G-BKVT
PA31 Chieftain: G-BFED, G-CITY, G-BGOX, G-LIDE
PA30 Twin Commanche: G-AVCY
PA28 Cherokee: G-ATWO, G-ATRR, G-ATMV, G-AZVV, G-ATON, G-BAKH, G-BAWK, G-BELR, G-BFWK, G-BGKS, G-BRME, G-SEJW, G-BRZP, G-BSHP, G-BOAH, G-KAIR
Cessna 150: G-AWUU, G-BCTW, G-BBTZ, G-BCBX
Cessna 172: G-AWPU
BN Trislander G-WEAC, G-BEFO

Passenger and Freight Figures

Year	Passengers	% Change	International Passengers	Freight/Mail Tonnes	Comments
1957	284,099		n/a	3,678	Nutts Corner
1958	269,566	-5.4	n/a	4,058	
1959	323,755	16.7	n/a	5,676	
1960	428,533	24.5	n/a	8,584	
1961	515,704	16.9	n/a	6,450	
1962	585,239	11.9	n/a	7,736	
1963	661,834	11.6	n/a	9,264	Aldergrove
1964	771,657	14.2	n/a	11,205	
1965	873,407	11.6	n/a	14,723	
1966	1,008,024	13.4	n/a	30,238	
1967	985,265	-2.3	n/a	23,073	
1968	984,096	-0.1	n/a	24,825	
1969	1,047,188	6.0	n/a	25,472	
1970	1,100,000	4.8	n/a	25,314	
1971	1,116,000	1.4	n/a	20,600	
1972	1,189,000	6.1	n/a	25,803	
1973	1,300,000	8.5	n/a	21,300	
1974	1,223,731	-6.2	n/a	21,200	
1975	1,185,000	-3.3	n/a	14,432	
1976	1,088,000	-8.9	n/a	15,040	
1977	1,039,411	-4.7	n/a	18,898	
1978	1,173,094	11.4	97,800	20,104	
1979	1,409,436	16.8	108,900	20,598	
1980	1,447,677	2.6	143,000	21,619	
1981	1,399,480	-3.4	183,000	22,458	
1982	1,442,420	3.0	230,000	24,547	
1983	1,411,704	-2.2	250,000	29,164	BIA
1984	1,622,324	13.0	300,000	35,169	
1985	1,668,234	2.8	300,000	32,964	
1986	1,881,667	11.3	400,000	35,935	
1987	2,177,710	13.6	500,000	32,967	
1988	2,174,629	-0.1	450,000	42,339	
1989	2,201,310	1.2	420,000	41,259	
1990	2,289,758	3.9	410,000	39,456	
1991	2,170,173	-5.5	350,000	39,842	
1992	2,248,128	3.5	500,000	38,756	
1993	2,117,795	-6.2	520,000	42,828	
1994	2,039,000	-3.9	622,000	36,538	
1995	2,346,000	13.1	654,000	41,449	
1996	2,351,000	0.2	676,000	39,236	
1997	2,459,000	4.4	673,000	37,700	
1998	2,627,000	6.4	818,000	38,883	
1999	3,013,025	12.8	949,233	40,459	
2000	3,200,000	5.8	1,000,000	46,000	estimated

The total passengers for BFS 1963 to 2000 stands at 60,287,843

Notes

1 *Ordnance Survey Memoirs of Ireland, Vol 35*
2 Author interview
3 *Belfast Telegraph*, 21 December 1918
4 Ibid
5 Ibid
6. W Sholto Douglas (MRAF Lord Douglas of
   Kirtleside), *Years of Combat*, Collins, 1963, pp 352–3
7 *Northern Whig*, 3 May 1919
8 Ibid
9 Ibid
10 Ibid
11 KE Hayes, *A History of the RAF and USNAS in Ireland
   1913–1923*, Irish Air Letter, 1988
12 Ibid
13 Ibid
14 *Flight*, 30 June 1921
15 Sir Alan Cobham, *Skyways*, Nisbet and Co Ltd, 1925, p 112
16 *Belfast Newsletter*, 23 June 1921
17 Ibid, 6 December 1922
18 *Belfast Telegraph*, 22 September 1922
19 Ibid
20 Ibid
21 Ibid
22 Cobham, p 290
23 *Belfast Telegraph*, October 1923
24 Ibid
25 Ibid, 5 October 1923
26 Cobham, p 291
27 *Belfast Telegraph*, 26 March 1926
28 *Northern Whig*, 3 July 1923
29 *Belfast Telegraph*, 10 July 1933
30 Ibid
31 Ibid, 31 May 1933
32 Ibid
33 *Belfast Newsletter*, 31 May 1933
34 Ibid
35 *Belfast Telegraph*, 31 May 1933
36 Peter Clegg, *Sword in the Sky*, Author's Publication, 1990
37 Ibid
38 Ibid
39 *Imperial Airways Staff News*, 22 August 1934
40 Norman Franks, *Scramble to Victory*, Kimber, 1987
41 Larry Forrester, *Fly for your Life*, F Muller, 1958
42 *Belfast Telegraph*, February 1938
43 Ibid

44 Ibid
45 Andrew Boyle, *No Passing Glory*, Collins, 1955
46 Ibid
47 *Skylines*, 1986
48 Ibid
49 Donald Bennett, *Pathfinder*, F Muller, 1958
50 WS Churchill, *The Second World War*, Cassell, 1954
51 Author interview
52 *Belfast International Airport News*, December 1990
53 Air Display Programme, 20 September 1947
54 *Airfield Focus 23*
55 *Jane's All the World's Aircraft*, Fred T Jane, 1952
56 *Belfast Telegraph*, 9 December 1958
57 Ibid
58 *Belfast International Airport News*, Autumn 1998
59 *Belfast Newsletter*, 23 March 1960
60 Ibid
61 Author interview
62 *Belfast Newsletter*, 26 October 1961
63 Ibid
64 Jonathan Bardon, *A History of Ulster*, Blackstaff Press, 1996
65 *BEA Magazine*, October 1963
66 Ibid
67 *Belfast Newsletter*, 26 September 1963
68 Ibid
69 *BEA Magazine*, November 1963
70 Ibid
71 *Belfast Newsletter*, 13 May 1965
72 Author's archives
73 Global Brochure, 1969
74 *Belfast Newsletter*, 14 October 1972
75 Air Fair Spectacular Programme, 1984
76 Belfast International Airport Annual Report 1991/92
77 BA statement
78 Robin Eames, text of sermon
79 *Ulster Airmail*, August 1995
80 Ibid, July 1996
81 TBI Annual Report, 1996
82 *Ulster Airmail*, July 1997
83 Ibid, February 1998
84 CO 230 Squadron

Sources & Bibliography

Primary Sources

Air Fair Spectacular Souvenir Programme

Belfast Airport Official Handbook, 1980

Belfast International Airport Annual Report, 1984/5, 1985/6, 1986/7, 1987/8, 1988/9, 1990/1, 1991/2, 1992/3, 1993/4, 1994/5, 1995/6

Belfast International Airport Handbook, 1983, 1984, 1986, 1987, 1988

Belfast International Airport Visitors Guide, 1988

Belfast International Airport Educational Guide, 1990

TBI plc Annual Report, 1996, 1997, 1998

Timetables: Belfast Airport, Belfast International Airport, British Airways, British European Airways, British Midland, Derby Airways, Air UK, British United, British United Island Airways, British Island Airways, Cambrian Airways, Aer Lingus, Air Ecosse, Air Ulster, Emerald Airways, Malinair, UTA.

Articles

'Aer Lingus and Belfast', *Irish Air Letter*, 1995

Lee, Jim, 'Aer Lingus 1936–1996', *Aviation Ireland*, January 1997

Negus, Geoffrey, 'Northeast Airlines', *Air Pictorial*, March 1971

Syal, Rajeev, article in *Sunday Telegraph*, 21 February 1999

Newspapers

Belfast Newsletter
Belfast Telegraph
Northern Whig
Sunday Telegraph
The Times

Periodicals

Air Pictorial
Aviation Ireland
BEA Magazine
Belfast International Airport News
British Airways News
Flight
IAFA Link
Imperial Airways Staff News
BIA Magazine
Irish Air Letter
RAF News
Skylines
Ulster Airmail *

*Articles by G Adams, R Andrews, R Bishop, S Boyd, R Burrows, E Cromie, E Franklin, J Hamilton, P Martin, P Myers, T Neill, G Warner, B Wilson, J Woods. This monthly journal of the Ulster Aviation Society, now 32 years old, provides a unique archive of raw material for those interested in aviation in Ulster and indeed beyond.

Books

Airplane – the Complete Aviation Encyclopaedia, Orbis, 1991–93

Bardon, Jonathan, *A History of Ulster*, Blackstaff Press, 1996

Barnes, CH, *Handley Page Aircraft since 1907*, Putnam, 1976

Bennett, Air Vice Marshal Donald, *Pathfinder*, F Muller, 1958

Bilsland, Bobby, Boyd, Stephen and Woods, Jack, *Ulster Aviation Handbook*, Adleader Publications, 1993

Boyle, Andrew, *No Passing Glory*, Collins, 1955

Brodie, Malcolm, *The Tele: a History of the Belfast Telegraph*, Blackstaff Press, 1995

Burge, Squadron Leader CG, *The Complete Book of Aviation*, Pitman, 1935

Butler, PH, *An Illustrated History of Liverpool Airport*, Merseyside Aviation Society, 1983

Byrne, Liam, *History of Aviation in Ireland*, Blackwater Press/Folens, 1980

Cameron, Dugald, *Glasgow's Airport*, Holmes McDougall Ltd, 1990

Chant, Chris, *Modern Jetliners*, Phoebus Publishing, 1980

—, *Turboprop Airliners*, Phoebus Publishing, 1980

Clegg, Peter, *The Quiet Test Pilot*, Author's Publication, 1989

—, *Sword in the Sky*, Author's Publication, 1990

Cobham, Sir Alan, *Skyways*, Nisbet and Co Ltd, 1925

Connon, Peter, *An Aeronautical History of the Cumbria, Dumfries and Galloway Region (Part II)*, St Patrick's Press, 1984

Corke, Alison, *British Airways: the Path to Profitability*, Pan Books, 1986

Corlett, John, *Aviation in Ulster*, Blackstaff Press, 1981

Cramp, BG, *British Midland Airways*, Airline Publications, 1979

Cranitch, Tom (ed), *What's the Date?*, Aer Lingus, 1986

Cross, Roy, *The Fighter Aircraft Pocketbook*, Batsford Ltd, 1962

Cruddas, Colin, *Cobham: The Flying Years*, Chalford, 1997

—, *In Cobhams' Company*, Cobham plc, 1994

Day, Angelique, McWilliams, Patrick and English, Lisa (eds.), *Ordnance Survey Memoirs of Ireland 1833–38, Vol 35, Parishes of County Antrim XIII*, Queen's University of Belfast, 1996

Donne OBE, Michael, *Pioneers of the Skies*, Short Brothers plc, 1987

Douglas, W Sholto (MRAF Lord Douglas of Kirtleside), *Years of Combat*, Collins, 1963

Flackes, WD, *Northern Ireland: A Political Directory*, Ariel Books, 1980

Forrester, Larry, *Fly for your Life*, F Muller, 1958

Franks, Norman, *Scramble to Victory*, Kimber, 1987

Gardiner, Geoff, *Airfield Focus 23: Aldergrove (Belfast)*, GMS Enterprises, 1995

Gillies, JD and Wood, JL, *Aviation in Scotland*, RAeS Glasgow Branch, 1966

Green, William, *The Observer's Book of Basic Aircraft – Civil*, Frederick Warne, 1967

Gunston, Bill, *Diamond Flight*, Henry Melland, 1988

—, *Early Jetliners*, Phoebus Publishing, 1980

Halliday, Ricky-Dene, *World Airline Colours of Yesteryear*, Aviation Data Centre, 1992

Hayes, KE, *A History of the RAF and USNAS in Ireland 1913–1923*, Irish Air Letter, 1988

Hooks, Mike, *Shorts Aircraft*, Chalford, 1995

Hutchison, Iain, *The Story of Loganair*, Western Isles Publishing Co, 1987

Jackson, AJ, *British Civil Aircraft 1919-59 Volume I*, Putnam, 1959

—, *British Civil Aircraft 1919-59 Volume II*, Putnam, 1960

—, *De Havilland Aircraft since 1909*, Putnam, 1962

Jefford MBE, Wing Commander CG, *RAF Squadrons*, Airlife, 1998

Kniveton, Gordon, *Wings of Man*, The Manx Experience, 1997

Lo Bao, Phil, *An Illustrated History of British European Airways*, Browcom Group, 1989

McIntosh, RH and Spry-Leverton, J, *All-Weather Mac*, Macdonald, 1963

March, Peter R, *Civil Airliner Recognition*, Ian Allan, 1995

Marriott, Leo, *British Airports Then and Now*, Ian Allan, 1993

Merton Jones, AC, *British Independent Airlines Since 1946*, LAAS/Merseyside Aviation Society, 1976–77

Nesbit, Roy, *An Illustrated History of the RAF*, Colour Library Books, 1990

Oram, Hugh, *Dublin Airport – the History*, Aer Rianta, 1990

O'Rourke, Madeleine, *Air Spectaculars – Air Displays in Ireland*, Glendale, 1998

Parsons, Ron and Watson, Alan, *Flying the Red Hand*, Bound Biographies, 1998

Phipp, Mike, *A History of Hurn Airport*, RAeS Christchurch Branch, 1991

Pickering, Graeme (ed.), *Military Aviation Review – United Kingdom 1999*, MAP, 1999

Quinn, John, *Wings Over the Foyle*, WWII Wreckology Group, 1995

Ryder, Chris, *The RUC: A Force Under Fire*, Mandarin, 1989

Scholefield, RA, *Manchester Airport*, Sutton Publishing Ltd, 1998

Share, Bernard, *The Flight of the Iolar*, Gill and Macmillan, 1986

Simons, Graham, *The Spirit of Dan Air*, GMS Enterprises, 1993

—, *De Havilland DH86 "Express"*, GMS Enterprises, 1996

Staddon, TG, *History of Cambrian Airways*, BA Museum Collection, 1979

Stroud, John, *Railway Air Services*, Ian Allan, 1987

Swann, John, *40 Years of Air Transport in Northern Ireland*, Ulster Folk and Transport Museum, 1971

Taylor, JWR, *British Airports (1964 edition)*, Ian Allan, 1964

Thetford, Owen G, *abc Airports and Airliners (1948 edition)*, Ian Allan, 1948

Warner, Guy and Woods, Jack, *Flying from Malone*, Colourpoint Books, 2000

—, *In the Heart of the City*, Adleader Publications, 1998

White, Molly O'Loughlin, *Belfast - the story of Short's Big Lifter*, Midland Counties, 1984

Woodley, Charles, *Golden Age: British Civil Aviation 1945–1965*, Airlife, 1992

Wright, Alan J, *British Airports (1991 ed)*, Ian Allan, 1991

Index

Italics indicate an illustration of or relating to the subject matter.

2 Squadron 5–6
4 Squadron 5
7 Squadron *96*, 97, 101, 124
9 Squadron 23
10 Squadron 59
24 Squadron 14
33 Squadron 76
43 Squadron 1, 30
48 Squadron 3, 32
52 Squadron 24
59 Squadron 36
72 Squadron 72, *74*, 82, 103, *104,*
86 Squadron 36
100 Squadron 5
102 Squadron 29
118 Squadron 47, *48*, 51
120 Squadron 36, *36*, 37, *43*, 45, 47–8
139 Squadron 24
201 Squadron 14
202 Squadron 39, 41, *41*, 59
206 Squadron 33
220 Squadron 36, *36,*
230 Squadron *77*, 100, *100*, 122
233 Squadron 33
245 Squadron 30–1, *30,*
252 Squadron *32*
254 Squadron 32
272 Squadron 33
275 Squadron 47
311 Squadron *33*, 34
407 Squadron 37
422 Squadron 37
501 Squadron 80
502 Squadron 11, 13–14, *13–14*, 18, 21, *22*, 23–4, *24*, 26, 28–9, 38–9, *39*, 42, *43*, *46*, 47, 92
518 Squadron 38, *38*
602 Squadron 14

617 Squadron 29
651 Squadron, AAC 47
655 Squadron, AAC *123*, 124
665 Squadron, AAC *123*, 124
774 Naval Air Squadron 82
845 Naval Air Squadron 82
846 Naval Air Squadron 124, *124*

ABC Carriers 85, 90, 95
Aberdeen 50, 81, 87, 93, 122
Aberdeen Airways 95
Abbotsinch 62, 64
Achilles HMS, 23
Aer Lingus 50, 58, *58*, 65, *66*, 67–8, 72, 76, 81, *82*, 85, 87, 104, *106*, 113, 126
Aero Films Ltd 6
Aeromaritime 72
Agriculture Ministry of 60
Aintree 8
Air 2000 104, *105*, 116
Air Ambulance 22, 81, 127
Air Anglia 84
Air Atlantique 90, 93, 119
Air Belfast 104, *104*, *106*, 107, 113
Air Bridge Carriers 117
Airbus A300 91, 94, 126
— A310 94
— A319 126
— A320 *95*, 97, *105*, *116*
— A321 *120*, 122
— A330 104 *106*
Airbus Industrie 91
Air Caernarfon 116
Air Canada *86–7*, 87, 101
Air Club 113, *113*
Air Council 15
Aircraft Acceptance Park (AAP), No 16 11
Air Display 14, *15*, 39, 51, 116
Air Ecosse 87, 90
Air Europa 98, *114*, 116

Air Express Company 6
Air Fair Spectacular 91, *91*
Air Force Cross 24, 26
Air Force One 107, *108*
Air France 95, 98, *99*
Airlines of Britain Group 113
Air Malta 85, *85*, 87
Air Ministry 1–2, 4–5, 10–11, 21, 35, 50–1,
Air Observation Post 47
Air Observers School (No 3) 27
Air Portugal 85
Air Safaris 58
Air Spain 75, *76*
Airspeed Ambassador 41, 57–8, *60*, 61, 65–6, 68
— Consol 39
— Ferry 15, 18, *18*
Air Support Command 72
Air to Surface Vessel (ASV) radar 29, 39
Airtours 87, 104, *105*, 113, *114*, 116, *116*, 122
Air Traffic Control (ATC) 49, 52–3, 87
Air Transat 98, 113, *113*
Air Transport Auxiliary 34
Air Ulster 68, *68*, 73
Air UK 84–5, 88, 90, 92, 102, *112*, 113
Air Wales 84
Airwork Ltd 21
Alcock, John 11
Aldergrove 1–8, *3, 5, 7,* 10–19, *11, 15*, 21–3, 25–32, *29,*
    34–45, *45–6,* 47–56, *50, 53,* 59–61, 63–6, *67,*
    68–72, 75–6, 79–82, *80–2,* 84, *86,* 88, *89,* 90–2, 95,
    96, 97, *99,* 102–3, 107, 116, *117,* 118–9, 122, *123,*
    124
Alexandra Park 4
Alitalia 41
Alma Ata 110
American Trans Air 98, 101, 113, *115*
Amery, Julian *55*
Amsterdam 18, 85, 102, 113, 125–6
Andover (place) 3–4, 23
Andover (aircraft) 64, 72
Anglo-Irish Treaty 5
Ann Street (Belfast) 25
Antonov AN124 110, *110*
Antrim (town) 2, 4, 12, 17, *17*
—, Co *28,* 61, *74, 104*
—, Glens of 17
Antrim Princess 82
Ardglass 31
Ards Airport 21–2, *21,* 40–1, *47*

Ards Peninsula 12, 24
Armagh 12
Armament Practice Camp, No 1 34, 37
Armament Training Camp, No 2 26
Armament Training School (ATS), No 1 27
—, No 2 26–7
Armistice 2
Armstrong Siddeley Lynx (engine) 16
Armstrong Whitworth Argosy 65, *65,* 72, 85, 90
— Whitworth Whitley 27–9, *29,* 39
Army Air Corps (AAC) 72, 47, *123*
Arras 1
Ashton, JD 12
Associated Airways Joint Committee 40
Astazou (engine) 62
Atlantic Ocean 11, 14–15, 23, 28–9, 31–4, 39, 41–2,
    44, 69, 75
Augusta Bell Jet Ranger 116
Auster AOP6 47, *47*
Australia 10, 15, 21
Autair 68, *68*
Auxiliary Air Force Squadron 24
Avair 87, 90
Aviaco 75, 80, 87
Aviation Advisory Council 49
Aviation Trader ATL98 Carvair 58
Aviogenex 80, 87
Avro 504 2, 6, 11, 15
— 548 6
— 618/Ten 16, *17*
— 642 18, *19*
— 748 58, *58*
— Anson 27–9, *28,* 31, 40
— Lancaster 17, 35–6, 45, 75
— Lincoln 39, 43, 45
— Nineteen 40
— Shackleton 17, *43,* 45, *45,* 47–8, *48*
— Ten 14, 16, 18
— Tutor 24
— Vulcan 17, 51, 91
— York 40, 60
Ayrshire 18

BAC 1-11 63–5, *63,* 72–3, *73–4,* 75, *78,* 79, 85, *90,* 91,
    98, 100, 102, 104, *104, 106, 118,* 119, 122
BAe 146 *94,* 95, 100, 108, *112,* 113, *120,* 122
— Advanced Turboprop (ATP) 95, 98, *99,* 102, 104, *104*
— Concorde 88, *89,* 91, 93, 98, *99*
— Jetstream 31 100, 102, *112*

— Jetstream 41 *119*, 122
— RJ-100 122
BA Express 103, *112*, 113, *119*, 122
Balbo, General Italo 14
Baldonnel 1, 5, 16
Balkan Airlines 80, *81*, 87, 116, *116*
Balmoral (Belfast), 6
— Showgrounds 14
Ballycastle 25
Ballyhalbert 31, 38, 49
Ballykelly see RAF Ballykelly
Ballykinler 6
Ballymena 61
Ballymoney 92
Ballyquillan 1
Ballyrobin 1
Bamberg, Harold 59
Bangor 12–13, *22*, 92
Bann, River 1, 12
Barclay, Capt David 22, 40
Barnard, Capt FL 6–7
Barton 19
Battle of the Atlantic 32–4, 39
Battle of Britain 3, 30
Battle of Britain Air Display 51
Bauman, Sgt Vaclav 31
BEA Magazine 51, 53
Beamish, Flt Lieut Victor 23–4
Bedford, Duchess of 7
Beechcraft King Air 127
Beinn na Lice 103
Belfast 1–3, 5–8, 10–22, 24–5, *27*, 30, 32, 35, 40–3, *46*, 47, 51, 54, 58, 60–3, 65–6, 68–9, 71, 75, 79–81, 85, 88, *89*, 92, 95, 99–101, *101*, *103*, *106*, 107–8, *108–9*, 117, *118*, *121–2*, 122, 124–5, 127
Belfast Airport 49, *50*, 55, *56*, 72
Belfast Blitz 31, 34
Belfast City Airport 99, 122, 125–6
Belfast Corporation 8, 21
Belfast Harbour Airport 34, 40, 49, 54, 90–1
Belfast International Airport 88, 91, *92*, 102, 104, 116, 118–9, 124, *125*, 126
Belfast Lough 8, 18, 23
Belfast Newsletter 6, 16, 50, 61, 72
Belfast Telegraph 2, 7, 8, 10–11, 15–16, 26, 49–50, 88, 98, *99*
Belfast Tradesmen's Social Club 69
Belgium 6
Bell & Co, SD 25–6, *25*

Bennett, Capt Donald CT 31–2
Bettington, Wing Commander AV 5–6
Billing, Flt Lieut Philip 28
Birmingham 7, 18–20, 24, 40, 57, 66, 75, 79, 81, 95, 98, 100, 102–3, 108, 111, *121*, 122, 125
Birmingham European Airways 97–8, 100, 102
Birmingham Executive Aviation 97
BKS Air Transport 41, 57, 61, 64–6, *64*, 68, *68*, 73
Blackburn Botha 29
— Buccaneer 51
— Roc *26*, 27, 30
— Shark 27, 30
— Skua 27, 30
Blackpool 14, 22, 24, 40–1, 58, 68, 87
Blake, Major 10
Bland, Lilian 70
Bleriot 4
Blue Eagles 104
Bodmin 4
Body, Edward (Ted) 34–5
Boeing 91
— 707 61, 65, *66*, 68–9, 72, 76, *76*, 85, 87–8, 107, 110
— 720 85
— 727 85, *85*, 100, 108, *109*, 111
— 737 79, *79*, 85, *94*, 95, *96*, 97–8, 102, *121*, 122, 125–6
— 747 69, 73, 81, *82*, *86*, 87, 93, 107, 113, *113*, 122
— 757 88, *89*, 93, 98, 102, *105*, 115
— 767 98, 102, 113, *114*
— B17 Flying Fortress II 36, *36*
— B29 Superfortress 45
— C-137 107
— Chinook *96*, 97, 101, *101*, 103, 124
— Stratocruiser 41
— VC-25A 107, *108*
Bombardier 122
— CRJ-200 *121*, 122
— CRJ-700 *121*, 122
Bomber Command 28
Bombing and Gunnery School, No3 27, 30
Boston 76, 104, *106*
Bournemouth 4, 58, 64
Boyle, Andrew 29
Bradford see Leeds/Bradford
Brancker, Sir Sefton 10
Bristol 41, 57, 79, 81, 84, 99, 100, 113
— Beaufighter *32*, 33–4
— Beaufort *33*, 34
— Blenheim 24, 27, 32–4, *34*

— Bombay 27, *27*
— Britannia 41, 59, *59*, 61, *61*, 68, *68*, 72, 75, *76*, 87
— Bulldog 23–4, 27
— Fighter 3, 5–7
— Freighter 41, 93
— Sycamore 47, *48*, 51
Britain 31, 35, 53, 55, 92, 97
Britannia Airways 72, 79, *79*, 87, *96*, 97–8, 102, 113
British (townland) 1
British Air Ferries 90
British Air Services Ltd 65
British Airtours 87
British Airways (BA) 22, 52, 77, 79–81, *80*, 84, 88, *89–90*, 91–3, 95, 97–8, *98–9*, 100, *106*, 107, *119*, *121*, 122, 125–6, *125*
British Caledonian 76, 79, 100
British Eagle International Airlines 59
British European Airways (BEA) 1, 22, 40–1, 49–52, 54–5, 57, 59, *60*, *63*, 64–5, 67, 75, 77, 82, 91–2, 98, 116–7
British Island Airways (BIA) 73, *73*, 84
British Isles 2–3, 16, 50, 76
British Midland (British Midland Airways, BM) 60, *60*, 65, *65*, 72–3, 75, *78*, 79–81, *82*, 84–5, 88, *90*, 91–2, *94*, 95, 98, 100–2, 104, *120*, 122, 125,
British Overseas Airways Corporation (BOAC) 17, 40–1, 59, 61, 67–8, *67*, 72–3, 75–7, *76*, 79
British United Airways group 58
British United (CI) 53, 63–4, 68
British United Island Airways (BUIA) 68, 73
British World Airlines 111, *111*
Britten Norman Islander 88, *92*, *96*, 97, 100, 124
— Norman Trislander 88, 111, *111*
Broad, Hubert S 7
Brooks, Keith 118
Brown, Lieut Arthur Whitten 11
Brown, TF 55
Browning machine gun 30
Brussels 122, 126
Brymon Airways 100, 102, 125–6
Brymon European 100, 102
Bundoran 15
Business Air 104, *105*, 111, 113

Caledonian Airways 61, *61*, 73, *78*
Caledonian/BUA 75
California 2, 31
Callard, Sqn Ldr 42
Cambert Field *69*
Cambrian Airways 41, 57, *57*, 65, *65*, 68, 77, *78*, 79

Cambridgeshire 23
Campbeltown 14, 16–17
Canada 31, 72, 102, 113, *113*
Canadair C-4 Argonaut 60
— CL-44 79, *80*, 95
Canadian Pacific 41, 61
Cape Town 10
Capitol Airways 41, 75
Cardiff 41, 57, 79, 81, 84, 99, 122, 125, *125*
Carlisle 8, 40, 60
Carrick -a -rede *74*
Carrickfergus 18
Carter, Gp Capt I Bonham 6
Carter, Robert 51–2
Carvair 58
Casement Aerodrome (see also Baldonnel) 1
Castle Archdale 37
Castle Bromwich 18–19
Castle Donington 60, 75
Castle Kennedy 41
Cavehill 8
Central Band of the RAF 46
Central Forecasting Office 41
Cessna 404 88
Chance Vought Corsair 37, *37*
Channel Express 92, 108, *109*, 111, 124
Charles de Gaulle Airport 88, *99*
Cheshire Homes 29
Cheshire, Leonard 29
Chester 6
Chicago 14
Christmas Island 45
Churchill, Sir Winston 32
Cierva autogyro 14
City Hall (Belfast) 6, *46*
City of York 6
Civil Aviation, Department of 5
—, Ministry of 49–50
Civil War (Irish) 5
Clare, Co 32
Clifden 11
Clinton, Bill and Hillary (Mr and Mrs) 107, *108*, 122
Clonmel 15
Coastal Command 28, 40, 45, 59
Coastal Patrol Flight, No 4 29
Coastguard 100
Cobham, Alan 6–8, 10, 15–16
Cold War 45
Coleraine 12, 23, 92

Collinstown 1, 5–6
Cologne 108, 111
Community Express *112*, 113
Concorde see BAe Concorde
Coningsby see RAF Coningsby
Consolidated Liberator 35–6, *36*, 40
Control Tower (Aldergrove) 42, 55, 87
Convair CV-990 Coronado 87
Copenhagen 60, 125–6
Cork 15, 62
Cornwall 39, 88
Costa Brava 72, 75
Coventry 108, 111
CP Air 87
Cricklewood 2–4, 6
Croydon 6, 8, 19–20, 40, 52
Crumlin 1, 8, 127
Culmore 14
Cushendall 17
Czech Republic 31

Daily Graphic 6
Daily Mail 6
Daily Mirror 6
Daily News 10
Daily Sketch 6
Dan Air (Davies and Newman) 60, 72, 75, *76*, 85, *85*, 87,
  90, 91, 97, 99, 100
de Havilland Aeroplane Hire Service 6–7
de Havilland (DH)4 6–7
DH4A 6, *7*
DH6 2
DH9 5–8, *9*
DH9c *5*, 6, 8, *9*, 10
DH16 7
DH50 7–8, *8*, 10
DH80A Puss Moth 15
DH83 Fox Moth 15–16
DH84 Dragon *17*, 21–2
DH86 19, *20*, 21–2
DH89 Dragon Rapide 21, 116
— C-2 Beaver 72, *72*
— C-6 Twin Otter *87*, 88, 90
— C-8-300 125
— C Dash 8 100, *125*
— Comet 50–1, *63*, 64, 72, 75, *76*
— Gipsy Moth 14
— Heron 41, 53, 55, 61–2, *61*
— Mosquito 39, *39*

— Tiger Moth 29, 35, 39
— Vampire 39, 42, *43*, 47, 80
Delphinus 21
Derby Airport 58
Derby Airways 53, 58, 60
Derry 12, 62
Derrygimbla 11
Derry Maid 68
Desoutter air taxi 14
Deutsche BA *106*, 104
Diamond Service, British Midland 91
Diana 19, 21
Didsbury 5, 10
Dieppe 39
Digby see RAF Digby
Divis Mountain 5, 18
Dominican Republic 119
Donaghadee 6
Donegal Bay 42
Donegall Quay 6, 14
Donnelly, Harry 110
Dornan, Jim 102
Dornier 17 31
— 228 93, *93*
Douglas C-47A Dakota 40–1
— C-117 53, *53*
— DC-3 Dakota 40–1, 53, 58, 60, *60*, 62, *62*, *65*, 67, *68*,
  82, 90, 95, 119, 122
— DC-4 58, 60
— DC-6 41, 62, 72
— DC-7 62
— DC-7C 41, 61
— DC-8 61, 68–9, 72, 75, *86*, 87, 93, *93*, 101, *101*
— DC-9 80–1, *82*, 87, *90*, 91, 95, 98, 100
— DC-10 69, 73, 79–80, 87, 113
Douglas, Sholto 1–2, 5, 30
Down, Co *12–13*, 21, *21–2*
Downpatrick 6, 12, 92
Drexel 4
Dublin 1, 4, 6–7, 15–16, 58, 61–2, 81, 87, 95, 101, 125
Dublin Airport 1, 72
Dundalk 15
Dundonald 13
Dungannon 12
Dungiven 19
Dunstable 41–2
Duxford 23

Eames, Archbishop Robin 103

Earhart, Amelia 14
Easons 7, *9*
East Midlands Airport 60, 65, *65*, 73, 79, 95, 100, 102, 104, 111, 125
easyJet 119, *121*, 122, 125–6
Edinburgh 3, 41, 58, 68, 79, 84, 87, 100, 111, *119*, 122
Edinburgh, Duke of 46, 124
Eglinton 62, 68
Eire 7, 42
Elizabeth (New Jersey) 15
Elizabeth I, Queen 1
Elizabeth II, Queen 46
Embraer Bandeirante 88, 90, 102, *102*, 111
— ERJ-145 125, *125*
Emerald Airways 61–3, *61–2*, 67–8, *69*, 70, *109*, 110, 124
Emerald European 102, *103*
Emerson, John 108
Empire Air Day 22, 28
England 2, 5–7, 10, 14, 29, 34, 36, 40–1, 63
English Electric Canberra 42–5, *44*, 51, 80, 82
— Electric Lightning 45, 51
— Electric TSR2 45
Enniskillen 12, 15, 60, 62, *77*, 122, *122*
Enniskillen 104, *104*
Environment, Department of the 75
Erne, Lough 62
Essex 18
Essex Air Port 19
Eurojet 107, 116
European Aviation 119
Euston 2
Everest, Mount 23
Exeter 58, 64, 68, 88

Fairey Battle 24, 26, 30
— Gordon 27
— Hendon 27
— Swordfish *26*, 27, 30
Falcon Holidays 101
Farman 4
Farnborough 6
Faulkner, Brian 50–1, 73
Ferguson, Harry 70
Fermanagh, Co 6, 12, 92
Fighter Command 30, 39–40
— Sector HQ 30
Flanagan, Sir Jamie 79
Fleet Air Arm 27, 37, 51
Fleetwood 5

Flight 6
Florida 102, 113, 119
Focke Wulf Condor 32–3
Fokker F27 Friendship 50, 58, *58*, *84*, 85, 90, 122
— F28 Fellowship *84*, 85, 95, 104
Fokker 50 97
Fokker 100 104 *106 112 120* 122 125
— FVII 16
— FXXII 40
Fox, Dudley 55
Foyle, Lough 14
—, River 12
Foynes 32
Frankfurt 126
Freestone, Paul 119
Fresson, Capt EE 13
Frogley, Syd 37
Futura 116

Gallahers 60
Galway, Co 11, 15
GA Monospar 14
Gander 42, 44
Gardiner, Bob 62, 68
Gatow see RAF Gatow
Gatwick, London 50, 63, 66, 79, 81, 91, 100, 111, 126
Geddis, Alderman William 68
Gemini 39
Genair 87, 90–1
General Aviation (GA) 81, *126*, 127
Genesis 102
Genesis Business Park 127
Geneva 125
George V, King 6
Germany 2, 31, 40, 60, 64, 80
Gill Air (Gill Airways) 99, 102, 111, 125
Gillam, Denys 24–6
Gillan, Philip 2
Gilmour, A 14
Glasgow 8, 14, 16–19, 21–2, 24, 31, 40, 57–8, 62, 64, 66, 68, 75, 77, 79, *92*, 93, 98, *98–9*, 102–3
Glasgow Daily Record 31
Glengormley Gap 108
Global 72, 75
Gloster Gauntlet *23*, 24–5, 27, 34
— Gladiator 27, 34, *34*
— Javelin 45, 51
— Meteor T7 42, *43*, 45, 80
Gloucester, Duke of 22

G.N.R. 4, 50
GO 126–7
Good Fortune 59
Goodyear 51
Gordon, Maggie 49
Gould, Wing Commander LTN 21
Grand Central Hotel (Belfast) 13, 32
Grant, Tom 24, 28, 52–3, 87
Greece 34
Greig, Capt DM 6
Groomsport 13
Grumman Gulfstream 1 97
Grundig 51
Gulf War 103

Haig, General 1
Haiti 110
Haji-Iloannou, Stelios 122
Hall, FO 12
Hampshire 3, 23
Handley Page (HP) O/10 8
— O/100 2
— O/400 2–4, 12, 15
— V/1500 2–3, *3*, 12
— W10 15
— 33 15
— Dart Herald 58
— factory 2
— Frederick 2–3
— Halifax 35, 37–40, *38*
— Halton 40
— Hampden 34
— Harrow 27
— Hastings 39, 41–2, *41*, 59
— Herald 60, 68, *68*, 73, 90, 92, 108, *109*, 111, 124
— Heyford *22*, 23, 27
— Hyderabad 12–13, *13*
— Victor 51
Harbour Grace 14
Hartley, Sir Harold 19–20
Haskett, Flt Lt 42
Hatchett, FW 6
Havana 93
Hawker Demon 22, 27
— Fury 27
— Hart 14, 24
— Hector 27
— Henley 26, *26*
— Hind 24, *24*, 27

— Hunter 45, 51
— Hurricane 27, 30–1, *30*, 34, 38, 44
— Tempest 44
— Typhoon 44
Hawker Sidderley (HS) 748 85, 97–8, *98–9*, *109*, 110
— Buccaneer S2B 103
— Trident 60, *60*, 64–5, *65*, *73*, 75, 79, 81, 85, *89*, 92, *92*
Heathrow, London 41, 52, 55, 57, 59–60, 64, 66, 79–81, 88, *89–90*, 91, 95, 102, 113, *120*, 122, 125–6
Hearne, Capt EDC 6
Heavy Conversion Unit (HCU), No 1674 36–7
Heavylift 59, 95, 113, 122
Heinkel III 31, 33
Helicopter Training and Hire (HT & H) 107, *107*
Helsinki 81
Hendon 6
Hertz 55
Hesketh, JR 18
Hess, Rudolf 31
Hibernian Airlines 62
Highland Airways 13, 40
Hillman's Airways 18–19, 21–2
Hillman, Edward 18–19
Hitler (Adolf), 31
Hoey, David 110
Holyhead 5
Hooton 18
Hooton Park 29
Hope, Capt Walter 8, 10
Hopkins, Sqn Ldr Martin 103
Hounslow 5
Hucknall 5
Hull 68, *68*
Humberside 87, 100, 102
Hunting Cargo Airlines 108, 111, 117
Hurricane *see* Hawker Hurricane
Hutchinson, Bertie 54

Iberia 91
ICI 51
Ilyushin IL18 87
— IL62 93
— IL76 95, 110
— IL86 95
Imperial Airways 6, 8, 10, 17–19, 21, 32
Imperial Airways Staff News 19
Instone Air Line Ltd 6
Inter European 98
'Interjet' route 63

Internet 122
Inverness 13, 103
Iona National Airways 95
IRA (Provisional) 76
Ireland 1–2, 4, 6, 10, 28
Irish Air Corps 1
Irish American Families Association (IAFA), 75
Irish Civil War see Civil War (Irish)
Irish Flight 5–6
Irish Free State 5
Irish Scot air service 17
Irish Sea 18–19, 28, 87–8, 108
Isle of Man 18, 20, 22, 24, 39–41, 57–8, 68, 79, 84, 88
Isle of Man Air Services (IoMAS) 22, 24, 40
Isle of Man TT Races 81
Italian Air Force 14
IT programme 73, 93–5, 113, 119

Jeffs, Gp Capt Jimmy 18, 52
Jersey 15, 41, 57, 79, 102
Jersey European Airways 85, 90, 100, *106*, 107, 118, *118*, 122
Johannesburg 110
Johnson, Amy 15
'Jumbo' jet 73, 81, *82*
Junkers 88 31
— Ju52/3m 40
Jupiter 19, *20*, 21

Keen, Allan 127
Keflavik 75
Kegworth 60, 95
Kehoe, Paul 119, 124
Kerry *106*, 107
Killead 1–2
King, Sir John 88
Kinloss 48
Kintyre 17
—, Mull of 103
KLM 18, 85, 102, *112*, 113, 102, *120*, 122, 125
Knight Air 102, *102*, 113

Lancashire 10, 45
Langford Lodge 1, 7, 49, 80, 97, 101, *101*, 103
Larne 1–2, 31, 82
Last Days 3
Lear, Bill 88
Lear Fan 88
— 2100 *88*

Learjet 88
Le Bourget 18
Leeds/Bradford 41, 58, 64, *64*, 66, 79, 84–5, 92, 102, *102*
Leisure International 113
Leopardstown 4
Limavady 12, 29, 37
Limerick 15
Lisbon 81
Lisburn 4
Liverpool 8, 18–19, 21–2, 24, 29, 32, 40, 50, 57–8, 65, 68, 79, 81, 84–5, 88, 100, 108, 110–11, 112, *113*, 125–6
Lloyd International Airways 75
LMS Railway Co 19
Lock, Capt JH 19
Lockheed C-5 Galaxy 107
— C-130 Hercules 72, 76, *77*
— L-749 Constellation 122, *122*
— L-1011 Tristar 69, 73, 79, *80*, *87*, 98, 113, *113*
— Electra 108
— Hudson 31–4, *32*
— Super Constellation 41, 62
— Vega 14
Logan, Jim 52, 80
Loganair 84, 87, 90, 103
London 2–6, 8, 14–16, 18–19, 24, 40, 52–3, 55, 60, 63–6, 68, 75, 79, 92–3, *93–4*, 95, 100, *104*, *106*, 117
Londonderry, Lady 18
—, Lord 14, 18, 21, 24
Londonderry 15, 62, 68
—, Co 14, 18
Long Kesh 37, 49
Lord, Cyril 15
Los Angeles 69, 80
Lossiemouth see RAF Lossiemouth
Lowe, Peter 59
Luce Bay 5
Luqa airbase 82
Luton 60, 75, 97, 102, 122, 126

MacDonald, Ramsay 18, 21
Mackie, Leslie 53
Macreth, Capt AJB 52
McAlister, WH (Billy) 50, 54, 56, 67–8
McAlister, Armstrong and Partners 50
McCausland's car hire 62
McClinton, Thomas 53
McClune, Ronnie 95
McCullagh, Sir Crawford 19
McDonnell Douglas (MD) F-4M Phantom 69

McDonnell Douglas (MD) F-4M Phantom 80 97
— 83 95, 98
McGarry, Henry 13
McIntosh, RH ('All-Weather Mac') 8, 10
McKeown, F 61
McLaughlin and Harvey 4
Maersk Air 102–3, *121*, 122, 125
Maia 32
Maintenance Command 59
Maintenance Unit (MU), No 23 27, 34, 37, *37*, 39, *44–5*, 45, 54, 59, 69, *69*, 80–2, 88
Majorca 75
Malinair *92–3*, 93, 95
Malet, Capt 18
Malet, Sqn Ldr HGR 18
Malone 8, 10, 21
Malone Air Park 8
Malta 34, 82
Manchester 4, 7–8, 19–21, 24, 40, 52–3, 57, 60, 66, 75, 79, 88, 100, 102, 104, *105*, *112*, 113, 126
Manx Airlines 88, 90, 104, *104*, 104, 113
Manx Airway 22, 58, 68, 102
Marchioness of Londonderry 18, *19*
Marconi 16
Marshal, Colin 88
Martin, Paul 88
Martinair 68, 72, 75
Mayhew, Sir Patrick 103
Mediterranean 102
Melrose, JD (Dougie) 74, 90
Menary, Geoff 60, 63
Mercury 19, *20*, 32
Mercury Airlines Ltd 53, 60
Messerschmitt Bf110 31
Meteorological (Met) Flight 23, *23*, 25–6, 34–5, *34*, 37, *38*, 39, 41, *42*
Michelin 51
Midland and Scottish (M & S) Air Ferries 14, 16, *16–17*, 18–19, 21, 40
Miles Aerovan 39, 62
— Messenger 39
Millisle 49
Milward, Anthony 49, 52
Missouri *69*
Mitchell, Brian 41, *42*
M'Kinlay Hay, FO 12
Mollison, Jim 15
Molyneaux, Lord 2
Monaghan, Rinty 39

Monarch Airlines 72, 87
Monkton 18
Montreal 32, 69, *121*, 122
Moore, Tony 80
Moscow 93
Mourne Mountains (Mournes) 12, 24, 56, 92
Mount Stewart 18, 21
Munich *106*, 107
Murphy, James 69

Napier Lion (engine) 2
National Aviation Day Display 15
National Flying Services 14
National Gallery (Dublin) 1
Neagh, Lough 1, 4, 6, 8, 12–14, 24, 26, *26*, 34–5, 37, 67, 87, 119
Nelson, Margaret 2
Nevada *88*
Newark 125
Newcastle (Co Down) 12
Newcastle (England) 40–1, 58, 66, 68, 79, 84, 97, 99, 102, 125–6
Newfoundland 11, 14, 31, 43
New Jersey 15
Newtownabbey 88
Newtownards 6, 12, 15, 21, *21*, 24, 34, 39, 41, *72*, 107, *107*, 116, 119, 122, *122*
Newtownstewart 12
New York 5, 65, 67–9, 75–6, 101, 104, *106*
New Zealand 3
Nicholson, George 22
NLM Cityhopper *84*, 85
North America 61, 73
North American Sabre F4 *45*
North Atlantic 14, 28, 31
North British Aviation Company 13
Northeast Airlines 73, 77
Northern Airlines 8, *9*, 10
Northern and Scottish Airways 22, 40, 52
Northern Ireland 6–8, 10, 22, 27, 32, 34, 40, 42, 45, 49, 51–2, 57, 61, 63, 68, 72, 75–6, 79, 85, 88, 90, 95, 99–101, 103, 107, 124, 127
Northern Ireland Airports Limited 75
Northern Ireland Tourist Board 65
Northern Ireland Transport Holding Company 75
Northern Whig 4, 8, 14
North of Ireland Aero Club 13
Northolt 40–1
North Sea 39, 81

North Weald 24
Norway 34
Norway, NS 18
Novotel Belfast International Hotel 101
Nutts Corner 40–1, 49–54, 56, 58–9, 69, 101, 117

'Old Fogey' 4
Omagh 6, 12, 124
O'Neill, Sir Neil 1
O'Neill, Terence 51, *67*, 68
Operational Conversion Unit, No 228 69
Operational Training Unit, No 9 34
'Operation Motorman' 76
Orangefield 6
Oranmore 15
Ordnance Survey report (1833) 1
Orkney 13
Orlando 69, 101, 116, 122
Orrell, JH (Jimmy) 16–17
Overseas National Airways 75, 79–80
Oxland, Sqn Ldr RD 11

Pacific Ocean 45
Pakenham, Lt Col 7
— family 1
Pan Am 41
Parcel Force 113, 119
Paris 18, 62, 72, 88, 95, 98, 100–1, 125–6
Paris Air Show 82
Park, Major Keith 2–4
Parsons, Flt Lt John 103
Pathe Freres 6
Pathfinder Force 32
Pelly, Nigel 18, 40
Pembroke 4, 42
Percival Gull 14
Phillips, Margaret 2
Phoenix Park 1, 7
'Pionair' class 41
Piper Aztec 70, *70*, 81
— Cherokee 70, *70*
— Navajo Chieftain 81, 88
Plymouth 4, 7, 28
Poole, Capt E 19
Portaferry 79
Portrush 15, 24
Post Office 85, 110
— Skynet 100
Pratt and Whitney Twin Wasp engine 40

Preston 10
Prestwick International Airport 18, 40–1, 61–2, 66, 68, 73, 79, 84, 87
Princess Maud 2
Prodger, Clifford 2

QUB Air Squadron 39
Queen Mother, Queen Elizabeth the 55, *55*, 56
Queen's Flight 46, 55, 64
Queen's Island 4

Rae, John 16
Railway Air Services (RAS) 18–22, *20*, 24, 40, 51, 54
Randalstown 12
Rangoon 10
'Rapiscan' 88
Rathlin Island 25–6, *25*, 28, 31
Reading 39
Red Arrows 91, *91*, 104
Redwood 2
Renfrew 14, 16–19, 40, 52, 64
Reno *88*
Robinson R22 107, *107*
— R44 107, *107*
Rolls Royce Eagle engine 2
— Griffon engine 40, 45
— Merlin engine 29–30, 39, 60
Rolson, Flt Lt 42
Rome 81
Romford 18
Rowson, AC 14
Royal 113, *114*
Royal Aircraft Factory BE2c 1, 6
Royal Air Force (RAF) 1, 3–7, 10–14, 17, 22–4, 26–32, *29*, 34–5, 37, 39, 41, 43, 45–7, *46*, 50–5, 59, 64, 68–9, 72, 82, 91, 100, 103–4, *123*
RAF Aldergrove see Aldergrove
— Ballykelly 37, 68, 72, 87, 92
— Coningsby 69
— Digby 5
— Gatow 82
— Lossiemouth 103
— Woodvale 41
Royal Auxiliary Air Force 46
Royal Dragoon Guards, 4th/7th 71
Royal Flying Corps (RFC) 1–2, 5, 10, 52
Royal Institute of British Architects 64
Royal Mail 81, 90, 108, 110–11, *111*
Royal National Lifeboat Institution (RNLI), *82–3*

Royal Naval Air Service (RNAS) 2, 5
Royal Navy (RN) 39, 82
Royal Ulster Constabulary (RUC) 47, 79, 100
Royal Ulster Yacht Club 13, *22*
Russell, AO 6
Russell, Gp Capt JC 23
Russell, Noel 49
Ryanair 119, 127

Saab SF 340A 111
Sabena *120*, 122, 126
Samson 59
'Sandeman's ghost', 37
Sanford 116, 119, 122
Saturn Airways 61
Saunders Roe Skeeter 47, *47*
Savoia Marchetti S55x 14
Scale Hall 5
Scotland 1–3, 8, 10, 22, 31, 39, 41, 87, 103
Scott, W 61
Scottish Air Ferries 14, 16
Scottish Airlines 40
Scottish Airways 40, 52
Scottish Aviation 41, 119
Scrabo Tower *21*
Seaboard and Western Airlines 41
Seacash 1
Search and Rescue 82, *82–3*
Seattle 69
Selway, Wing Commander John 50, 71, 75
Sempill, Col the Master of 15
Servisair Ltd 66, *66*, 95, 108
Shannon Airport 61, 65, 68, 76, 81, 85, 93, 95, 104, *106*, 126
Shetlands 81
Short Brothers (Shorts) *27*, 35, 43–5, 49, 88, 99, 111, 113, *121*, 122
Short S23C 32
— SA4 Sperrin 43, *43*, 44
— SB4 Sherpa 44, *44*
— SC5 Belfast 59, *59*, 72, 110, *110*, 113
— SD 330 88, 99, 101, 111, 127
— SD360 99, 111, 127
— Skyvan 61, 62, *62*, 75
— Stirling 34–5, *35*, 37, 39
— Sunderland 28, 37
— and Harland 27, 34
Short-Mayo Composite project 32
Shute, Neville 18

'Shuttle', BA, (also 'Super Shuttle') 81, 88, *89*, 91, 93
Sikorsky CH-53 Super Stallion 107
— MH-53 Sea Dragon 107
— VH-60 Seahawk 107
Silver, Arthur 75
Silver City Airways 41, 58
Simpson, Sqn Ldr 30–1
Sixmilecross 12
Skavsta Airport 124
Skylines 93
Slattery, Rear Admiral Sir Matthew 49
Smalls Lighthouse 42
Solway Firth 10
Sopwith 1½ Strutter 1
— Snipe 17
South Africa 15, 110
Southampton 64, 68, 88
Spacegrand 87, 90
Spanair 95, *115*, 116
Spantax *86*, 87
Spartan Cruiser 22
Speke Airport 18, 32, 40, 85
Spitfire see Vickers Supermarine Spitfire
Squire's Gate 40
Srom, Sgt Leopold 31
Standard Aircraft Corporation 15
St Angelo 60, *77*, 122, *122*
Stanley, Jean 51
St Anne's Cathedral (Belfast) 47, 103
Stansted, London 100, 104, *104*, *106*, 107, 110–11, 118, *118*, 122, 126–7
Stapleford 19
St Colmcille 81, *82*
Stead Air Force Base *88*
Stephens, Laura 7
Stephens, Solomon 7
Sterling Airways 75
Stewart, Edward 17
St George's Channel 28
St John's 11
St Louis *69*
Stockholm 124
Stockton, NR 52
Stoke-on-Trent 24
Stokes, Bob 108
Stormont 14, 51, 73
Stornaway 39
Strangford Lough 92
Stranraer 1–2, 8, 41

Streamline Aviation 85
Strike Command 82
Sud Aviation Caravelle 75, *75*, 85, 94
Sumburgh 50
Superb 111, 116, *117*
Supply, Ministry of 43
Surinam Airways 93, *93*
Swann, John 52
Sweden 17
Sword, John C 16–18, 21
Sydenham 15, 24, 34, 40, 43, 49, 59, 88, 90
Sydenham Avenue 35

Tarom 87
TAC Heavylift see Heavylift
TAT 95, 98
Taylor, Denis 59
TBI 118–19, 124, 127
Teeside Airport 50, 61, 68, *68*, 87, 91, 125
Tennyson, Lord 4
The Times 6–7
Thompson, Adam 73
Thurley, Ralph 51
Tiree 38
Titan Airways 111
TNT *94*, 95, 108, *109*, 111
Toogood, Flt Lt 12
Toomebridge 61
Toronto 69, 75, 81, 88, 125
Tower Air 107
Trade and Industry, Department of 75
Transeuropa 85
Transglobe 61
Translift 101, *101*
Trident see Hawker Sidderley (HS) Trident
Treasury 75
Trenchard, Marshal of the RAF Lord 11
Triezennes 1
Tuck, Bob Stanford 24
Tupolev TU-134 80, *81*, 87, *110*
— TU-154A 80, *81*, 87, 98, *116*
Turner, Alderman WG 8
Tyrella beach *13*
Tyrone, Co 12

U-boats 28, 32–3, 35–6, 39
U-93 29
U-206 39
Ulster 2, 4–6, 8, 11–13, 16–17, 22, 46, 49, 51–2, 61, 67,

69–70, 75, 91–2, 101, 127
Ulster Airmail 101, 118–9
Ulster Air Show 116
— Air Weekend 119
Ulster Aviation Ltd 39
Ulster Aviation Society 70, 82, 88, 92, 97, 101, *101*, 103,
    108, 113, 119
'Ulster Flight' 72
'Ulster Flyer' 41
Ulster Maid 68
Ulster Maple Leaf Club 69, 101
'Ulster Milk Lift' 41
Ulster Motor Show 41
Ulster Transport Authority 50
Ulster Workers' Council strike 79
United Airways 22
United Kingdom (UK) 22, 39–40, 55, 64, 66, 75, 79, 81,
    95, 102, 122, 126
Unst 81
Upper Air Unit 37
USA (United States of America) 31, 88, 113, *113*, 125
USAAF 40
US Navy 53, *53*
UTV 50

V1 flying bomb 44
Vacations Ireland 104, *106*
Vancouver 68–9
Very Long Range (VLR) aircraft 35–6
Vickers Merchantman *74*, 75, 90, 108, 111, 116, *117*
— Supermarine Southampton 14
— Supermarine Sea Otter 39
— Supermarine Spitfire 22, 30, 34–5, 38, *38*, 40, 104, *104*
— Valiant 44–5, 51
— Vanguard 50, 52–5, *53–4*, 57, 64–5, *74*, 75, 77, 87, 117
— Varsity 82
— VC-10 61, *67*, 68, 72, 93
— Vildebeeste 22
— Viking 41, 46, 58, 82
— Vimy 11–12, *12–13*, 92
— Virginia 13–14, *14*, 21–3
— Viscount 41, 49–50, 52–3, *53*, 57, *57*, 59, *63–4*, 64–5,
    65, 68, *68*, 72, *72–3*, 75, *78*, 79, 84–5, 90, 94, 111, *111*,
    113, 119
— Wellington 22, 28, *33*, 34, 37, 41
Victoria Cross 29
Vienna 125
Virgin Express 127
Viva 98

Volkert, GR 2

Wales 2, 39, 57
Wales, Prince of 14
Wardair 72, 87
Warton 45
Waterford 15
Welford, Capt John 65
West Country 57
Western Desert 34
Western Front 3
Westland Aerospatiale Gazelle 82, *123*, 124
— Aerospatiale Puma 76, *77*, 82, 100, *100*, *123*, 124
— Bell 47G Sioux *70*, 71, 82
— Lynx 82, 104, *123*, 124
— Scout 71, *71*, 82
— Sea King 82, 124, *124*
— Wallace *22*, 23, *24*, 25–7, *26*
— Wapiti 14
— Wessex 21, 71–2, *71*, *74*, 82, *82–3*, 103, *104*, *123*, 124
Westminster 49, 51
Wheeler, Rosemary 53
White, TE 19
Whitehall Securities 22
Whitelaw, William 75
Willis, Gerry 80–1, 90, 94
Wilson, Bob 41
Wilson, FG 110
Windsor Castle 88
Wood, AB 19
Woodgate Aviation (Executive) *69*, 70, 81, 85, 90, 111, *111*
Woodgate, Mike 61, 63, 70–1, *70*, 81, 97, 127
Woodley Aerodrome 39
Woodvale see RAF Woodvale
Workman, Capt 4
World Airways 69, 72, 113, *114*
World War One 15
World War Two 34, 42, 75
Wynne-Eaton, George 35

Yorke, Rosenberg and Mardell 50

Other aviation titles by Colourpoint:

Flying from Malone
Belfast's First Civil Aerodrome
Guy Warner with Jack Woods
1 898392 63 3   £4.99   32pp pbk
210 x 148mm   8 b/w photos & 7 lineart.

In the mid 1920s, Belfast was at the forefront of the development of civil air transport in the British Isles, and an adventurous move by Belfast City Council established the first municipal aerodrome in the United Kingdom at Malone.

This book pays tribute to the pioneers and innovators whose bold efforts paved the way for the global commercial aviation network that exists today.

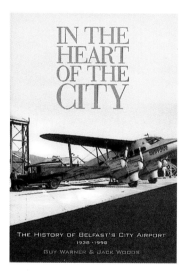

In the Heart of the City
The History of Belfast City Airport
Guy Warner & Jack Woods
0 948124 91 1   £4.99   64pp pbk 218 x 148mm
20 b/w 32 colour photos + 2 maps.

Northern Ireland has a remarkable aviation history which, arguably, began in 1910 with the first flight to Ireland made by Henry Ferguson in a 40hp monoplane.

The outbreak of the First World War led to the development of both Aldergrove and the short lived Malone Aerodrome and, in 1928, another route was pioneered between Liverpool and Belfast Harbour. This new route was to be the nucleus for the development of Belfast City Airport, and *In the Heart of the City* shows how the airport has developed over the past 60 years.

Anyone who is encouraged by reading this book to take a deeper interest in aviation in Northern Ireland, past and present, is urged to join the Ulster Aviation Society.

The Society may be accessed through the Colourpoint website at **www.colourpoint.co.uk**, or by telephoning the Society directly on **(028) 9445 4444**.